Günter Bayerl Padilha

AFRICAN MATRIX TERREIROS

Günter Bayerl Padilha

AFRICAN MATRIX TERREIROS

A MAPPING IN BOA VISTA - RORAIMA

Imprint

Any brand names and product names mentioned in this book are subject to trademark, brand or patent protection and are trademarks or registered trademarks of their respective holders. The use of brand names, product names, common names, trade names, product descriptions etc. even without a particular marking in this work is in no way to be construed to mean that such names may be regarded as unrestricted in respect of trademark and brand protection legislation and could thus be used by anyone.

Cover image: www.ingimage.com

This book is a translation from the original published under ISBN 978-620-2-56128-0.

Publisher:
Sciencia Scripts
is a trademark of
International Book Market Service Ltd., member of OmniScriptum Publishing Group
17 Meldrum Street, Beau Bassin 71504, Mauritius
Printed at: see last page
ISBN: 978-620-2-70785-5

TABLE OF CONTENTS

INTRODUCTION

Current issues relate to the Amazonian context and to the Amazon region. One such connotation is that the Amazon is a space occupied by indigenous and traditional populations, thus completely forgetting the existence of black populations in the interior and in the urbanizations that have rapidly transformed the Amazonian reality in recent years.

The invisibility of black populations in the Amazonian context is a central concern of this investigation, which is motivated to seek in the cultural manifestations of the region the presence of an Afro-Brazilian expression. We know that the Amazon since the "Rubber Cycle" in the 19th century until the most recent mining activities, has been the recipient of a mass of migrants who brought with them their traditions and beliefs. In addition, there are significant remnants in the region of slave labor that used African labor in their commercial activities, which today are known as the remnants of Quilombos.

In the late 1970s and early 1980s, with the expansion of garimpo in Roraima and the construction of the BR 174 connecting Boa Vista to Manaus - A. M. and, consequently, to the Northeast and other regions of the country, it is the beginning of the migratory flow from Maranhão to the state. Therefore, it is from this period that the presence of Afro-Brazilians in Boa Vista is registered, mainly in the peripheral neighborhoods of the city.

The question is: Are there Umbanda and Candomblé Terreiros in Boa Vista? How many? Why aren't they visible?

The search for this answer takes place in the primary observation of the social dynamics and cultural manifestations that exist in the city of Boa Vista such as the carnival and the capoeira rodas that denounce the existence of a cultural expression closely linked to Afro-Brazilian roots. However, it is not enough to perceive the existence or non-existence of an Afro-Brazilian population in Boa Vista, it is necessary to preliminarily diagnose which aspects favor the invisibility of this population niche that conforms to the good urban society. Thus, the first chapter will address African cultural evidence and ideological pressures that deny and devalue the construction of an Afro-Brazilian identity in Brazil and, consequently, in the Northern Region.

In order to better understand the Afro-Brazilian cosmovision in Boa Vista, the religious bias of Candomblé and Umbanda is based on two manifestations of resistance and syncretism that result from the historical process of a productive activity based on the slavery of Africans. Thus, the second chapter will bring, in general terms, the founding elements of Candomblé and

Umbanda in order to have an idea of what can be found in the third stage of the investigation, i.e., the location and mapping of the existing Terreiros in Boa Vista.

The third chapter brings the experience of the fieldwork, from the first stage of locating external aspects that denounced the functioning of an African matrix terreiro de religião, that is, a white flag hoisted on bamboo, to the results of conversations with the fathers and mothers of Santo to get to know the particularities of each of the 21 terreiros that were located, identified and mapped during the period of the research, which began in the second half of October 2006 and was completed in the second half of March 2007.

With this work, we see that Afro-Brazilian cultural expression is present in Boa Vista through the Terreiros de Candomblé and Umbanda, mainly in the periphery of the city, where they are an instrument of conservation and transmission of knowledge and traditions vital for the continuity of their existence as Afro-descendants. There is a blatant invisibility of the terreiros in the municipality of Boa Vista, which makes it very difficult for them to organize and articulate the struggles so that their rights are guaranteed.

CHAPTER I

1. A LOOK: IMPRESSIONS, RESTLESSNESS AND ANALYSIS OF CULTURAL ASPECTS OF AFRO-DESCENDANTS.

When I arrived in Boa Vista on February 2, 2002, I carried in my imagination that the North Region was an immense green sea inhabited by indigenous, riverine and migrants. Walking through the streets of Boa Vista, I tried to identify in people physical and cultural characteristics that would prove my imaginary. But soon I realized that Roraima had more cultural riches than my imaginary of a migrant from the south could encompass. Of course, in the foreground, one could observe the dispute for indigenous lands, which reveals the political and cultural importance of the indigenous people who inhabit the state. In the background we can observe the importance of migration to Roraima, specifically in the period of the 1980s, the peak of mining.

The second plan of my observing eyes, which sharpens my curiosity and invites me to enter the Federal University of Roraima - UFRR, in the course of Social Sciences, so that I can find answers to why my indigenous imagination of the Northern Region was not confirmed. But, even so, it was this imaginary that was reinforced outside the state. Understanding this second plan was the great goal of my studies. But I soon realized that there were many details that needed to be elucidated, for example: why are migrants pasteurized and homogenized as if migration were taking away their unique cultural and ethnic characteristics? Why is the migrant necessarily seen as an ally of the local oligarchy in the struggle for occupation of indigenous lands? Why is there no mention of afro-descendants as a specific group that contributes to the construction of the state of Roraima?

From readings and observations through the streets of Boa Vista is that the last question takes into account my scientific concern. I have been able to observe shy cultural manifestations of Afro-descendants, for example, the Carnival held here, which is a caricature of Rio de Janeiro's Carnival and is also influenced by the Manaus' Ox. We see some capoeira rodas being played in the squares, but there is not an afro musical expression like axé that exists in Bahia, but there is the reggae sung by the afros immigrants from the Cooperative Republic of Guyana and a shop for religious articles for the Candomblé and Umbanda cults that reveals the probable existence of terreiros. There is no effective political organization of the Negroes.

These findings point to two situations in which Afro-descendants live in Roraima: the first is that Afro-descendants exist but do not become visible; and the second is society's denial of their existence.

This process of invisibilization demonstrates how Afro-Brazilians, even though they have contributed substantially to shaping Brazilian culture, are still politically and economically disadvantaged in relation to other ethnic groups. It also reveals that for the elite of Brazilian society, specifically in our case, the Roraima oligarchy, it is important to deny Brazil's Africanity (Cf. DAVIS : 2000, p 14).

It seems that Brazilians ignore the historical facts that have made the majority of the Brazilian population linked to African traditions. For, throughout the period of the slave trade, Brazil received a large contingent of African ethnic groups to serve as labor in the plantation and sugar cane mills located in the Northeast Region[1]. But other regions also received Africans to be used in mines, coffee plantations and cattle raising (Cf. LOPES: 1988, p 140-141). São Luís, Recife, Salvador and São Vicente are the main slave ports.

Another fact that has gone unnoticed by Brazilians throughout history is that both the Northeast and the North depended on slave labor coming from Africa. But these slaves resisted the slave economic model by fleeing. Thus they formed Quilombos and others were welcomed by indigenous tribes where they established relations with the Indians and sometimes became tribal chiefs and once wizards. The proof of the black presence in the Amazon is historically verified at the time when Ceará and Amazonas declared, in 1844, that all slaves were free (Cf. DAVIS : 2000, p 32).

The current testimony of the Afro presence in the North of the country are the struggles for land ownership of the remnants of quilombos, especially the high Rio Trombeta, in Pará. It is these quilombolas that possess the memory of the past of the mocambos,[2] individual narratives that agree with the collective memory of freedom, abundance, respect for elders and relations with local commerce that confirm that the black communities in the North Region have historically been silenced. For in the imaginary countryside the Amazon is not a space for black populations, but this imaginary is forgotten that Óbidos, Alenquer, Santarém have their origins in the quilombolas that escaped from the farms. (Cf. FUNES : 11.12.06)

---

[1] Nina Rodrigues reports that the monarchic government claimed that Africans seized from trafficking ended up spontaneously preferring to stay in Brazil rather than be exported and today one can find several groups, mainly in the states of Bahia, Pernambuco and Maranhão. P. 100 – 120.

[2] Mocambos, thus, were called the black slaves and fugitives who inhabited the Amazon.

Brazil officially abolished slavery in 1888, but many people of African descent remained in debt bondage and poverty. The end of slavery put Afro-Brazilians in a situation of landlessness, forcing them to migrate to urban centres and live in the favelas. Today, a substantial percentage of the peasants who fight for land are Afro-Brazilians in the movements of Rural Workers, Sem Terra and Quilombolas. The struggle for land in Brazil has an ethnic component to consider. To this exact point it seems that none of the historical facts contribute to the assertion that in Roraima there is a considerable afro-descendant population and apparently their invisibility could be sustained from the historical information provided above. However, there is a very important fact to be considered when analyzing the invisibility of Afro-descendants in Roraima. Historically, the lack of land and the scarcity of work in the rural areas of the Northeast have driven their inhabitants to migrate to other regions of the country, to the seringais and to the garimpos.

Thus, the state of Roraima received the vast majority of migrants after the opening of BR 174 in 1978 and the garimpo boom in the 1980s. According to IBGE (2000), in this period the population growth rate was 9.63%, the highest registered in the country. The Northeast Region of Brazil is the largest contributor to the demographic growth of Roraima with almost 32% and, specifically, Maranhão accounts for 23% of the total population of the state, of which almost 62% live in the capital. Bastide (1980) gives a precious hint of the ethnicity of this mass of migrants who arrived in Roraima when he states: "Black Brazil, which would be first of all the coast of the Northeast". Therefore, the search for visibilizing the afro-descendant, in Roraima, must be emphasized from the end of the 1970's and beginning of the 1980's when the great migratory flow of Maranhão's people to the state takes place.

Given that migration to the state of Roraima has a very high percentage of people of northeastern origin, who have historical ties with Africa, consequently, with a large percentage of Afro-descendants, the puzzle persists: why is there an invisibility of Afro-Brazilians?

Some important facts, which often go unnoticed when it comes to giving visibility to Afro-descendants, are that they have gone through a process of humiliation both in slavery and in the process of liberation, as Florestan Fernandes states:

> Blacks are living testimonies of the persistence of a destructive colonialism, disguised with skill and buried by unbelievable oppression (...) suffered all the humiliations and frustrations of slavery, of an abolition made like a revolution from white to white and of the resentments it had to accumulate, vegetating in the cities and trying to be people, that is, ordinary citizens. (FERNANDES : 1989, p 08).

The abolition of slavery brought social and political change to Brazil, as slave lords and the elite drunk with the ideals of the French Revolution equality, freedom and republic will command the nation's steps in this way:

> ("...) the Republic would solidify the dominance of the landowner and then engage in a national campaign to "Europeanize" Brazil, a campaign in which the "whitewashing" of the national population and the replacement of the African racial heritage by the European one would assume a prominent role. Intellectuals and politicians developed a set of government programs that aimed to transform Brazil into a European society in the tropics. In a series of "urban reforms", areas of the city centre dominated by colonial buildings and architecture were overthrown and rebuilt in the European belle époque style. The 1891 Constitution specifically prohibited African and Asian immigration to the country, and the national and state governments made the attraction of European immigration to Brazil a priority for national development. (ANDREWS : 1989, p 90-91)

Therefore, even if the greatest beneficiaries of abolition were the slaves, the post-abolition political referrals will hit blacks hard. This is because they will have to dispute the labor market with European immigrants in a situation of political inequality. Consequently they will have to sell their work at a lower price and they will have the most precarious working conditions in relation to European immigrants. This is the thesis that Fernandes defends:

> The blacks were "automatically" put aside in favor of the immigrants, who were more specialized, more imbued with a capitalist work ethic and had the most effective support from family and community solidarity structures (...) They simply did not have the skills to face the Europeans, concluded Fernandes - in specialized labor, trade or factory work (ANDREWS : 1989, p 119 and 121).

Certainly these situations experienced by the slaves are forging their low self-esteem and transmitting it to their descendants. Moreover, they receive from society the reinforcement of their inferiority when they explicitly demonstrate that they wish to whitewash the national population through miscegenation. In this sense, the idea of whitening contributes to making the afro-descendant invisible. The elite thought that with the European immigration of the 19th century and, consequently, the miscegenation would cause the gradual disappearance of black people from Brazilian society. This thought aggravated even more the situation of prejudice and racism in the country (Cf. HASENBARG : 1979, p 239). Thus, Florestan argues that the primary prejudice in Brazil was the belief that there was no prejudice (FERNANDES, apud Davis : 2000 p. 43).

The Afro-descendant, in the 1930s, suffered with Gilberto Freyre's standardizing speech of racial democracy.

> (...) because it "solved" state racism in a convincing way for whites (and even for a parcel of blacks) by silencing the possibility of a difference placed by blacks, since all Brazilians were converted into "equals" in this discourse of a false racial cordiality. (CARVALHO: 2004 p 5).

Carvalho's thought about the harm that the idea of racial democracy has brought to the Afro-descendant population is shared by Florestan Fernandes, who says:

> Democracy will only be a reality when there is, in fact, racial equality in Brazil and the black man does not suffer any kind of discrimination, prejudice, stigmatization and segregation, whether in term, class or race. (...) The fictitious racial democracy, whose function is to imprison the black man within paradoxes that lead to denial of himself, to constrain him to see himself as he thinks he is seen by whites (FERNANDES : 1989, p 24-26).

The multiculturalism existing in Brazil has been interpreted over time as an amalgam of the Brazilian people, where Indians, Europeans, Africans and Asians contribute to the formation of a mixed nation-state.

> On the ethical-cultural level, this transfiguration takes place through the gestation of a new ethnic group, which has been unifying, in language and customs, the Indians disengaged from their gentile life, the blacks brought from Africa, and the Europeans wanted here. It was the Brazilian who emerged, built with bricks from these matrices as they were being undone (RIBEIRO :   1995, p 30).

Both the ideas of Gilberto Freyre's racial democracy and the ideas of Darcy Ribeiro's cultural matrices contribute to the Brazilian people being seen as different, living together peacefully, because each Brazilian recognizes that he is the fruit of a miscegenation that characterizes him as Brazilian. These two ideas disregard the particularities of each ethnic group.

> The society was, in fact, a mere conglomerate of people, multi-ethnic, coming from Europe, Africa or natives from here, activated by the most intense mestizaje, the most brutal genocide in the decimation of tribal peoples and the radical ethnocide in the cultural decharacterization of indigenous and African contingents. Thus, paradoxically, ideal conditions for ethnic transfiguration are achieved by the forced disindianization of the Indians and by the de-fricanization of the black, who, stripped of their identity, find themselves condemned to invent a new inclusive ethnicity of all of them. This is how a growing human mass that had lost its face began to merge: they were ex-Indians who had been Disindianized, and above all, mestizos, black women and Indians, many of them, with a very few European whites who multiplied in them prodigiously (RIBEIRO : 1995 p. 448).

In this way, the Brazilian people would be in their essence a mestizo people who would be condemned to forget their cultural matrices and, consequently, should build a common identity of mestizo, that is, to structure an imaginary that embraces the whole nation.

> We, Brazilians, in this picture, are the people in being, prevented from being. A people of half-breed in the flesh and in the spirit, since here the half-breed was never a crime or sin. In it we were made and still are. This mass of natives from the mestizaje lived for centuries without self-awareness, sunk in *no one*. Thus, it was even defined as a new ethno-national identity, that of Brazilian. A people, until today, in being, in the hard search of its destiny. (RIBEIRO : 1995, p 453).

Following the thought of Darcy Ribeiro, the ideas of miscegenation make people lose the cultural references that identify them with a people, in this sense, the Afro-Roraimense would find himself at the epicenter of the search for a new identity that has no connection with the African, but is totally alien to himself. This, hypothetically, would take him away from the need to reaffirm himself as an Afro-descendant, just by reaffirming himself as a historical product of the ethnic mixture that places him in the condition of Brazilian. However, where is the preservation of primordial elements of his cultural matrix in this process?

Certainly there will not be a satisfactory answer to this question, but any formulation of hypothesis on the invisibility of the afro-descendant must have as a reference the process of formation of his imaginary by the Brazilian elite that in a veiled way reinforces the prejudice and discrimination against the afro-brazilian. In addition, the white elite take away from themselves the responsibility of solving the problem and attribute to class difference the fact that discrimination and prejudice exist in Brazilian society (Cf. HASENBARG : 1979, p 244).

In this way the afro-descendant needs to overcome the ideas of whitening, racial democracy and mestizaje that would supposedly lead him to have equal treatment within the social dynamic that would form the Brazilian people. He must also overcome his economic and social inferiority, the result of the historical exploitation of a slave system that did not indemnify him for his work time nor gave him conditions to be a landowner or a rural worker in order to then be visible as a citizen and a nation builder.

I believe that the invisibility of Afro-descendants in Roraima receives a special spice, the predominance and virulence of the conflict between "Indians" and "non-Indians" for the right to land, which so marks the recent history of Roraima (SANTILLI: 2001, p 47). However, this invisibility does not mean that there are no Afro-descendants in the state and that they do not cultivate their traditions and beliefs. For this reason, it is necessary to carefully observe the data offered by IBGE in order to realize the existence of afro-descendants and make them visible to Roraima society.

Brazil has the second largest black population in the world, second only to Nigeria. Thus, Brazil is important for African-American history (ANDREWS : 1998 p 21). But according to data from the last IBGE census (2000), only 10,554,336 Brazilians identify themselves as "black", that is, 6.2% of the population. In addition, the number of people who declare themselves black is 65,318,092, which makes up 34.4% of the national population who identify themselves with black people. In the state of Roraima there are 199,661, or 61.5% of the population who identify themselves as full-brown and only 13,715 people, or 4.2% of the population who recognize themselves as black. This is a surprising observation and an enigma about the invisibility of the black population in Brazil. However, determining who is black in Brazil is quite complex. The historian Décio Freitas states that in Brazil "we consider as blacks all those who present a dark pigmentation of skin, a pigmentation that is neither white nor Indian" (ANDREWS : 1998 p. 384). Race scholars in Brazil and the black movements tend to group blacks and browns as people of African descent (ANDREWS ; 1998 p. 21). Following the concepts mentioned above, the Afro-Brazilian population in Roraima would reach the percentage of 65.7%.

Many indigenous groups that inhabit Roraima are registered as mulattoes. However, not all grizzlies are afro-descendants. There are indigenous people who have declared themselves to be brown. I understand and know how contradictory and complex the color item is in the IBGE survey. For this reason, we will not enter into this discussion because we have no way of affirming how many indigenous people are self-declared grizzly, so we have chosen to follow the argument presented by Andrews that the black movement groups blacks and grizzlies with being afro-descendants.

Reflecting on the data from IBGE and the possible interpretations that can be given to them, it is clear that they represent only a reflection of the almost "invisibility" of blacks in Roraima, being another and, perhaps more important, the surprising rarity of afros cultural evidence (music, clothing, traditions, cuisine) in this state that is opposed to other parts of Brazil, especially in the Northeast, where the cultural presence is of paramount importance for the construction of the identity of "blacks. Among these, without a doubt, the Afro-Brazilian religiosity plays an important role. Has the whitening ideology of the Liberal Republic, post-abolition, associated with Gilberto Freyre's thought of Brazilian racial democracy found resonance in the Afro-Brazilian population of the state to the point that it denies its African origins? Was it only the "white" and "brown" northeasterners who migrated to Roraima[3]? Is there the possibility of migration "causing" a loss of "black" identity (self-identification) in migrants? Or is it that along the migration there is a loss of cultural traditions, proper to the northeastern blacks, which makes them "less visible" in the Roraima context, facilitating a conscious or unconscious "change of identity" in them?

Faced with these questions, I decided to dedicate myself to identifying and documenting the Afro-descendant presence in Boa Vista through its religious expressions, that is, the simple location of Candomblé[4]and Umbanda[5]terreiros . This is because I consider them key institutions for a black or afro-descendant identity.

> Nevertheless, on the philosophical level, we can point out an aspect that gives unity to the peoples of traditional Africa: the individual is considered alive because he has an ascendant (he is someone's son or grandson), and who falls to guarantee him or her the memory of his or her life and existence is the perspective of his or her descendant (his or her future son or grandson). (...) The existence of the individual is translated through his or her being-self (which implies time and space or place) in the world, through daily life, work or leisure, always connected to the social, cosmic, natural and supernatural universe to the same time, being impossible to separate what is concrete and spiritual, or to determine what is sacred or profane, in the life of these peoples (MAE; USP: s/d).

I believe that the philosophical aspect of the continuity of African peoples contributes to their customs and traditions remaining alive throughout history, through a system of transmission that goes from generation to generation. In this way, Afro-descendants preserve their culture and change their traditions when it suits them so that contact with their ancestors is not lost.

---

[3]I believe I have good reason to rule out this possibility beforehand. Throughout the northeast the black population predominates and from this region are the majority of migrants who arrived in Roraima, almost 32% of the general population of the state (IBGE 2000). It would therefore be expected that self-declared "blacks" should be present in greater numbers among northeastern immigrants in Roraima. But if we consider the discussion presented by Andrews and the practices of social movements in adding the mulattoes and blacks to measure the afro-descendants (Andrews 1998, p.21) we can consider that Roraima is an afro state, with 65.7% of the population having African ancestry.

[4]Terreiro de Candomblé is a sacred space identified with the white flag hoisted by a bamboo at a height above the roof of the terreiro. The terreiro incorporates in its logic of division of the physical space countless cosmological conceptions concerning the sacred and the profane, the mystery, the sacred and the religious power. This is because in candomblé, spaces and objects have axé, a vital force that can be conserved, handled and transmitted. The terreiro is considered a living being, which must be honored with rituals, sacrifices. In the terreiro there are special initiation rooms, altars, places where certain deities are "planted", a place for sacrifices and space for plants, because Candomblé needs to have contact with the lócus nature of axé. For this reason, the terreiro is often called "roça" (SILVA : 2000, p 95-106). The kitchen is important in the terreiro, because it prepares the food of the children of the house of the Orixás, it is also a meeting point, because between one activity and another there is much talk about the food preferences of the gods, myths and traditions of Candomblé (LIGIÉRO : 2004, p 140).

[5] Cf. SANGIRARDI Jr (1988). The enclosures where the umbanda services are held are called "spiritist center", "terreiro", "tent" and "cabana".

Therefore, I suspect that Afro-Brazilian religiosity may be the gateway to understanding the cultural dynamics of Afro-descendants in Boa Vista, a city far from the great cultural nuclei traditionally afros of Brazil, such as the cities of Salvador[6] - BA and São Luís[7] - MA. But it received a considerable contingent of northeastern migrants after the second half of the 1970s, who probably brought in their luggage the religious traditions practiced in the Northeast.

> Besides Casas das Minas, the Casa de Nagô is also prominent in the capital of Maranhão, (...) In many terreiros of São Luis, vodun fasts have undergone an acculturation process with orixás nagôs, caboclos and catholic saints. Such process irradiated to the North region, in yards that, falsely, call themselves heirs of the Casa de Minas Maranhense. The babssuê, from Belém do Pará, constitutes a confusing amalgam of tambor-de-mina, candomblé-de-caboclo, catimbó, pajelança, popular catholicisms, spiritism and esoterism. The members of the sect affirm that the name "babassuê" derives from "Barba suera", being "Barba" apócope from "Bárbara", the name of a saint with great devotion in the terreiros of Maranhão. That is why babassuê, also called batuque-de-mina, is more commonly known as batuque-de-santa-bárbara. (SANGIRARDI Jr. : 1988, p 38)

Therefore, locating and mapping the Candomblé and Umbanda terreiros will be a possibility to prove that Afro-descendants keep aspects of the African philosophical imaginary. Thus, we will see if the terreiros can be concrete ways to give visibility to the afro-descendants who inhabit the state of Roraima and also verify if in fact the terreiro is an important space for the conservation of the afro-brazilian identity.

---

[6] Cf. Bleeding, Jr. (1988), The state of Bahia received Africans from the ethnic group Jeje-Nagô, Yoruba peoples
[7] Idem (1988), the state of Maranhão and the coast of Pará received Africans from the Banto ethnic group.

CHAPTER II

2. THE RELIGIONS WITH AFRICAN MATRIXES

In order to discover what is contained in the way of life and cultural manifestations of Afro-descendants in Roraima, I decided to get to know the religions with African roots that have taken root in Brazilian territory. In order to reach my goal of locating and mapping the Terreiros in the city of Boa Vista, I needed to know some aspects of Candomblé and Umbanda. So we have to do, in what follows, a journey through time to the African continent, from where men and women were plucked to be placed in a strange land. In this land, Brazil, its descendants have lost their identity, or rather, reformulated an identity of resistance, which has passed through spirituality.

2.1 - THE ORIGINS OF THE AFRO-BRAZILIAN CULTS.

When we think of Africa, we tend to consider it a unity in itself. But it is a complex political, ethnic and cultural division. For the purposes of this chapter we will point out that the millions of Africans who forcibly immigrated to Brazil came from different regions of Africa, and their languages, for the most part, belonged to two linguistic trunks: Yoruba and Bantu.

The influence of African civilizations on the formation of Brazil takes place mainly in the Northeast, since, according to Hasenbalg, until the end of the 17th century, the slave population was concentrated in the "sugar economic area", between Maranhão and Bahia:

> In 1538, the first African slaves brought by Portuguese ships arrived in Brazil. Despite being uniformly called black, the slaves belonged to different ethnic groups, coming from different African regions. But they were generally classified into two main groups: the Bantus (Congo, Angola and Mozambique) and Yoruba (Sudanese Jejes and Haussás). The Nagô-Iorubá people strongly influence Bahian life, with several members coming from high social class and priestly committed to the preservation of their traditions and religious precepts. (...) it is important to point out the coincidence between the dates of mass immigration from the Yorubas to Brazil, starting in 1830, and the fall of the city of Oyó, capital of the country Ioruba, defeated and devastated by the Daomé in 1935 (LIGIÉRIO : 2004, p 19).

With the commercial expansion of Europe's mercantile economy, especially the Portuguese one, the African continent became a major supplier of slaves to the colonies. According to IANNI (1988), from the beginning of the traffic of Africans in the 16th century until the end of slavery in the 19th century, 9,500,000 black people arrived in the American continent. Of these, 38% stayed in Brazil, 6% went to the United States of America, 17% were taken to the Antilles, 17% to the French Caribbean colonies, and 17% to the Spanish colonies. Temporally the flow of slaves is distributed as follows:

> 1451-1500 – 50.000
> 1601-1700 - 560.000
> 1701-1810 – 1.891.400
> 1810-1870 - 1.145.000 (CURTIN apud HASENBALG : 1979 p 128)

The slave trade between Brazil and Africa can be classified in four major cycles:

1. Guinea Cycle: Second half of the 16th century.
2. Angola Cycle -Congo: throughout the 18th century.
3. Costa Mina Cycle: until the beginning of the second half of the 18th century.
4. Benin Cycle: until the middle of the 19th century. (LODY apud AMARAL : 2003 p.39)

When the blacks arrived in Brazil and were taken to work on the farms, they needed to form a new community. The need to seek their axé1 became more necessary in Brazil than in Africa, as slavery took away from the black man much more than freedom. It deprived Africans of their families and their identity as a people, that is, it denied them the condition of human beings. Therefore, the tradition of the orixás remained strong in the new world:

> The African religions, in the new world, have acted from the beginning, as a true community center that takes care of the psycho-emotional balance of its components and that, through its millenary botanical medicine, takes care of the health of its members and leaves inheritances to the new generations through the indissoluble binomial art-religion (...) A situation of common misfortune, the struggle for freedom and the restoration of lost links with Africa were strong reasons to unite enemy ethnicities and traditionally rival nations.(LIGIÉRO : 2004 p 21-26)

In the colonial period, Africans could not worship their deities freely because, before embarking, they used to be baptized and collectively "converted" to Christianity. This caused enslaved blacks to resort to syncretism to continue their religious traditions:

> During the period of slavery in Brazil, blacks brought from Africa continued to worship their deities, bringing the sacred objects of African religion always hidden behind or under altars with images of Catholic saints, and doing their worship as if they were revering these saints, but with the intention of having more freedom to worship their orixás. Since the African religion and its sacred objects were unknown to most whites, they thought that blacks had already converted to Christianity (Amaral 2003 : p 35).

Understanding the dynamics of the process of arrival of Africans on Brazilian soil is of fundamental importance to understand the development of religions with African roots throughout the history of Brazil. Each cycle brings with it essential cultural elements for the differentiation of the Afro-Brazilian cult, as we will see below, when we approach Candomblé and Umbanda separately.

2.2 - CANDOMBLÉ.

The word candomblé has Yoruba origin and means literally: "dance". Originally Candomblé is a religious dance, which is danced by women2 called sambas. The function is to invoke the orixás so that they are incorporated into the initiated people. In Brazil, candomblé has come to define the cult of the orixás. (Cf. www. edeus : 30.06. 2005). It has a strong heritage of the Ioruba religiousness that cultivates the orixás, gods associated with the forces of nature. African polytheism has mixed with indigenous polytheism and the Catholic cult of saints. The ceremonies are divided into two parts: the first is a preparatory rite, with sacrifices and offerings to the orixás. The second is open to public participation. Songs of praise are sung to the orixás who are incorporated in the daughters of the saints, dancing in a circle to the sound of songs and atabaques (Cf. www. thecauldronbrasil : 30.06.2005).

In candomblé, sacrifices and offerings have the function of pleasing the orixás. From time to time, the person who is a fan of candomblé has the obligation to pay homage, and to make offerings to his or her orixás. These guarantee favors and the protection of the orixás. Sacrifice, as part of the cult of the orixás, goes back to the practices carried out by blacks in Africa in the cult of ancestors. According to Prandi:

> We can define the ancestor cult as the set of beliefs, myths and rites that regulate the bonds of a community with a large number of dead who have lived in that community and are linked to it by kinship, according to family lineages, believing that the dead have the power to interfere in human life, and should then be propitiated, placated through sacrificial practices for the welfare of the community. Through sacrifice, the ancestor shares in the lives of the living, sharing with them the fruit of successful crops, hunting, war and so on. Although every dead person deserves respect and sacrifice, it is the illustrious dead who place themselves at the center of the cult. They are the founders of the ancient family lineages, the conquering heroes, founders of cities, which includes the deceased belonging to the royal family, especially the king. **(PRANDI** : 30.06.2005).

For the adepts of candomblé, to render offerings to the orixás is to "feed" what is deepest in each being, is to assume and strengthen the set of characteristics of their orixás. For this reason, when a person of candomblé goes through difficult moments, he or she more than quickly goes and prepares offerings for his or her deities, in order to find help to solve their problems (Cf. AMARAL : 2003, p 40-41)

Within the Brazilian territory, candomblé has suffered influences from several cultures, mainly the indigenous and the Christian (western). This influence can be perceived through the material culture of Afro-Brazilian religions: crosses, chalices, scales and images of Catholic saints, as well as elements of indigenous culture are used.

2.2.1- THE ORIXÁS.

The African people, known as Yoruba, believed in impersonal supernatural forces (spirits) that they considered present in plant or animal objects, endangering human life (animism). They must offer sacrifices to placate the fury of these natural forces. Many of these spirits of nature were worshipped as deities and later were called orixás. (Cf. PRANDI, 30.06.2005).

Therefore, orixá is the generic name of the Yoruba divinities, holders of the cosmic forces and of nature: the axé. In the orixás the creative force, the whole and the infinite, that is to say, the universe, is manifested. The orixás have family bonds that establish a mythical basis for the existence of the people; their origin. (Cf. www.edeus.org. see also www.axeoya 30.06.2005)

For example, in the case of the orixá Ogum there is a direct relationship between agriculture and craftsmanship with iron, the production of agricultural tools, weapons of war, knives, machetes and swords. Ogum has become a God of metallurgy, war and technology, distancing himself, emblematically, from nature and approaching the world of social activities. With the passing of time and technological evolution, the orixás have been acquiring anthropomorphic forms, distancing themselves even more from nature. However, with the environmental concern and the preservationist consciousness of some leaders, the candomblé has been rescuing the initial connection of the orixás with nature, for example: in the figure of *onilé,* the owner of the earth, who represents our planet as a whole. (Cf. PRANDI, op. Cit.)

The most important power of the orixás is that of incarnating themselves, momentarily, in one of their "descendants" (faithful), and transmitting to them axé, protection and direction of their destiny. As such, the orixás assume the characteristic of a guardian of activities essential to life in society, and adherence to the cult of the orixás constitutes a lifestyle in which the cult is a substantial part.

2.2.2 - AXÉ, LIFE FORCE.

As this is an essential element for religions with African roots, we think it is appropriate to approach Axé in greater depth. The meaning of this word is "principle of life" or "vital energy". Everything that is divine creation has *axé* and can transmit it: human beings, animals, vegetables, minerals and objects.

> Ax is energy, a life force that dynamically constitutes and maintains the cosmic order. It concerns the small things of everyday life as well as the big decisions of life. It relates to the individual as well as to the community, it dynamizes both human beings and all of nature. Without the strength of axé, the whole system would not be dynamic. (BERKENBROCK : 1997, p 259).

Axé **is** life itself. On axé depends the existence, both individual and general; without axé, there is no possibility of the development of creation. As the bearer of axé, the human being has an individual and social responsibility. This means that each person is responsible for the active maintenance of the structures that shelter and protect life, i.e. the world. Axé is understood from a cyclic cosmovision. It makes the link between today, the ancestors and future generations ensure the historical continuity of the people. Thus, to be candomblecist means to be part of the history of a people that builds its identity from the commitment to life.

2.2.3 - AXÉ ON LEAVES.

The Yoruba gave importance to nature, plants, stones, rivers and lakes in their religious magic system. The Yoruba maxim is *"kosi ewê kosi orixá"*, which can be translated by: *"you can't worship orixás without using the leaves."* The candomblé currently practiced in Brazil preserves this maxim. It is believed that plants are sources of axé, without which there is no life or movement. Therefore, without plants there is no possibility to worship in candomblé grounds (Cf. PRANDI, 30.06.2005).

This information on the importance of leaves in African matrix cults is a valuable clue in this process of locating and mapping the terreiros. Investigating backyards with abundant vegetation may reveal the places where the orixás are cultured. This is because, in candomblé, certain plants have a wide use: to wash and sacralize objects, to purify the head and body of the priests, to cure physical diseases and to ward off all kinds of evil. However, it is not enough just to harvest the leaves in nature, prayers are needed for them to suffer the intervention of *Ossaim* and to release axé (Cf. PRANDI : op. cit. 30.06.2005).

2.2.4 - AXÉ IN MUSIC, BODY AND DANCE.

In several cultures, music and dance are central to the whole magical-religious universe. This is particularly true for candomblé. The chants chanted prepare the faithful to be possessed by the orixás. Thus, during the trance, the *holy daughter* becomes the orixá himself. Because the human being is seen holistically in candomblé, there is no division between spirit and body, earth and heaven. There is only the universe as a dynamic order full of axé that sets the cosmos in motion (Cf. BÁRBARA www.ffch.usp.br/sociologia/posgraduacao/jornadas/papers/,30.06.2005)

Music and dance are used to go back to the time of the myth, of the origin, the ancient harmony with the world. It is characterized by being danced in a circle in a counter-clockwise direction. The sacred circle reminds us of the time-space of the myth which, according to legends, refers to the ancient divinity of the earth. The dance is not pure displacement in space. The body moves, occupies a space structure, creates a personal space. The repetition of movements is perceived as a creation, each movement **gives origin to** the divinity and gives the possibility of returning in time and space. In the dances of candomblé, the feet are in continuous contact with the earth, to absorb its energies. (Cf. BÁRBARA : Op. Cit.).

The sound is a conductor of *axé,* so the *atabaques* are sacred instruments and receive *every year appropriate rituals*. They can only be played by special priests, the *alabés*, who learn the repertoire over time. *It is they who can call the community and, above all, the orixás to come down to the feast and close the feast with a special touch* (Cf. BÁRBARA : Op. Cit.).

To understand the close connection between music, dance and the experience of the believer, it is necessary to keep in mind that music and dance are perceived by all senses, not only through the ear and the look, but also through the skin, involving the believer as a whole. The body in candomblé is the temple of the sacred par excellence because it is considered as a receptacle of the orixá (Cf. BÁRBARA : Op. Cit.).

Thus, understanding that music is a determining factor in Candomblé, one can take it as a starting point to reach a place where there is a terreiro. Thus, when one hears the drum roll it is very likely that one is in front of a terreiro where, at that moment, a ritual is being performed for the orixás, where barefoot people are dancing in a circle, and under the action of their orixá.

2.2.5 - THE NATIONS OF CANDOMBLÉ.

The enslaved Africans belonged to several ethnic groups including the Ioruba, the Ewe, the Fon, and the various Bantus groups as groups that worship the orixás, they became relatively isolated in the different regions of Brazil, so they were formed into several "nations". The concept of "nation", employed in candomblé, is not political, but rather "identity" for those who participate in the cult of the orixás. The "nations" are distinguished from each other mainly by the set of venerated deities, the atabaque and the language used in the rituals.

There are currently three great "nations" of candomblé in Brazil, the "Nação Ketu", the "Nação Jeje" and the "Nação Angola". One of the differentiations between the three is the name of the one God, for the "Nation Ketu" is Olorum,   for the "Nation Bantu", Zambi, and for the "Nation Jeje", Mawu. (Cf. Wikipedia, 05.02.07).

There are still some differences in the classification of Candomblé "nations". This is why it is necessary to review two classification models: the first is presented by Wikipedia and the other by Lody:

- Nagô or Yoruba;
- Ketu or Queto(Bahia) and almost all states -(Ioruba or Nagô in Portuguese);
- Ketu or Efan in Bahia, Rio de Janeiro and São Paulo;
- Ijexá, mainly in Bahia;
- Nagô Egbá or Xangô of the Northeast in Pernambuco, Paraíba, Alagoas, Rio de Janeiro and São Paulo;
- Mina-Nagô the Mine Drum in Maranhão;
- Xambá in Alagoas and Pernambuco (almost extinct);
- Bantu, Angola and Congo (Bahia, Pernambuco, Rio de Janeiro, Minas Gerais, São Paulo, Goiás, Rio Grande do Sul), a mixture of Bantu, Kikongo and Kimbundo. (Wikipedia, 05.02.07).
- Ketu-nagô Nation (Yoruba);
- Nation Jexá or Ijexá (Yoruba);
- Nation Jeje (Fon);
- Nation Angola (Banto);
- Congo Nation (Banto);
- Nation Angola/Congo (Banto);
- Nation of caboclo (Afro-Brazilian model) (LODY apud Amaral : 2003 p 40)

In Brazil, each nation that cultivates the orixás preserves and transmits religious traditions brought from the African continent. However, in Brazilian territory the African religiosity has been meeting with indigenous and European expressions, resulting in a new Afro-Brazilian spirituality that made possible the emergence of "Umbanda".

2.3 - UMBANDA: ANOTHER BRAZILIAN RELIGIOUS EXPRESSION.

We are a multicultural and multiethnic country. Umbanda" is a religious expression that channels diverse cultures and ethnicities, it absorbs imaginary, practices and rituals from various cultural and ethnic segments of Brazilian society. It has as its dominant characteristic being Brazilian, because it is a convergence of elements of candomblé, Kardecist Spiritism of Shamanism and Christianity.

According to Saraceni (2003), Umbanda is:

> ...a spiritist and spiritualist religion. Spiritist because, in part, it is based on the manifestation of the guiding spirits. And spiritualist because it incorporated concepts and practices (...) such as spiritual and religious magic, ancestor worship, religious cult to the higher spirits of nature (...) preaches that the divinities of God (the orixás) are divine beings endowed with faculties and powers superior to those of the spirits and has in them its religious foundations, recommending the cult to them and the practice of offerings as a way of revering them, since it is inseparable from the earthly or divine nature of all that God created. (SARACENI : 2003, p 29).

The beginning of the Umbanda happened with the manifestation of the "Mr. Caboclo das Sete Encruzilhadas" in the medium Zélio Fernandino de Morais, event that occurred on November 15th 1908, when the latter attended a session of the Spiritist Federation, in Niterói:

> Zélio was invited to the table. (...) and when the work began, spirits manifested themselves as Indians and slaves. (...), Zélio felt dominated by a strange force and heard his own voice inquiring why the messages of the blacks and the Indians were not accepted and if they were considered backward only because of the color and social class that they declined. This observation almost caused a commotion. After all, one of the seers asked the entity to identify itself (...), If you want a name (...) that is this: I am the CABOCLO DAS SETE ENCRUZILHADAS, because for me there will be no closed paths. And, continuing, he announced his mission: to establish the bases of a cult, in which the spirits of Indians and slaves would come to fulfill the determinations of the Astral. The next day, he declared, he would be in the residence of the medium, to found a temple, which would symbolize the true equality which must exist between incarnate and disincarnate. (...) On the following day, November 16, 1908, at the residence of the young medium's family, at Rua Floriano Peixoto, 30 in Neves, district of Niterói, the entity manifested itself punctually at the scheduled time - 8 p.m. (...) In this meeting, the CABOCLO DAS SETE ENCRUZILHADAS established the norms of the cult, whose practice would be called "session" and would take place in the evening, from 8 pm to 10 pm, for public attendance, totally free (...). The uniform to be worn by the mediums would be all white, of simple fabric. No financial remuneration would be allowed for the service or for the work done. The chants would not be accompanied by atabaques or rhythmic clapping. To this new cult, which was founded that night, the entity gave the name of Umbanda, and declared the first temple founded for its practice, with the denomination of Our Lady of Mercy Spiritist Tent (?). (www.pegue, 25.01.2007)

This manifestation coincides with Brazil's historical moment that places it on the path of liberal evolution, based on the abolition of slavery in 1888 and the proclamation of the Republic (1898).

Umbanda is loaded with Christian ethics and reinterpretation of French spiritism. This syncretism seeks to keep Umbanda away from the African universe to such an extent that at the beginning of its structuring it was thought that its origin was in India.

> The First Congress of Spiritism in Umbanda, in 1941, in Rio de Janeiro, was a remarkable moment in this process. (...) One of the theses approved in the congress was the idea, somewhat bizarre, that Umbanda had its roots in India, from where it would have been taken to the African continent. The theses approved at the meeting tried, on the other hand, to connect Umbanda to Spiritism, which Allan Kardec, in France, in the middle of the 19th century, had tried to bring science closer. The Brazilian elite tended to value this free aspect of Spiritism. Some of the first intellectuals of Umbanda preferred to present it as a modality of Spiritism, reinterpreted in Brazilian soil and added a ritual, nonexistent in the French Kardec matrix. (ISAIA : 2006, p 28).

Umbanda's quest to distance itself from the practices of Candomblé and the African imaginary is evident in the posture taken by the first Umbandists of only working with the spirits of "caboclos", "old niggers" and "children" and did not admit in their meetings the manifestation of the orixás. The "caboclos" are "indigenous" spirits who help those in need. The "old blacks" have space in Umbanda because of their wisdom. (Cf. ISAIA : 2006, p 30)

There is an undeniable influence of spiritism on Umbanda:

> Adjusting to the Kardecist doctrine as to mediumship, Umbanda gradually replaces African deities with spirits, thus transforming the very meaning of African cultural tradition. The lack of a doctrinal unity made each terreiro elaborate with autonomy its own conceptions about doctrine and ritual. The greater or lesser influence of kardecism or Christianity will be determined individually by the priest of each temple (AMARAL : 2003, p 44).

This autonomy of each priest and the freedom in the doctrinal elaboration had its limitation marked by the foundation of Federations and the creation of rules with the objective of giving uniqueness to Umbanda:

> In 1937, the temples founded by the CABOCLO DAS SETE ENCRUZILHADAS came together, creating the Spiritist Federation of **Umbanda** do Brasil, later called União Espiritualista de **Umbanda** do Brasil. And in 1947, the JORNAL DE UMBANDA (UMBANDA'S JOURNAL) appeared, which, for more than twenty years, was a doctrinaire organ of great value. Zélio de Moraes installed umbandist federations in São Paulo and Minas Gerais (www.pegue, 25.01.2007).

As time went by, Umbanda was affirming her doctrine. Throughout the 40's to 70's, several reformers began to seek to give greater doctrinal consistency. However, as all things happen in its due time, Umbanda developed a singular capacity for syncretism, paying attention to social transformations and incorporating the orixás, carioca rascals, northeastern cattlemen and other spiritual manifestations.

Today no one disassociates Umbanda from Afro-Brazilian culture anymore. (Cf. ISAIAS : 2006, p 32). The diversity existing in Umbanda is not seen as a problem and, nowadays, the Umbanda terreiros follow, in a general way, the seven lines scheme of the orixás which is presented as follows: Oxalá, Iemanjá, Ogum, Iansã, Xangô, Oxossi and Cosme e Damião.

> Some lines are subdivided as follows: I hope it's in Old Black, Lines of Souls, Baianos. Iemanjá in Oxum line, Nana Line and Sailors Line. Oxossi in Caboclos da Mata Line and Boiadeiros Line. These Lines are called the right line3. Exu Line is called Left Line4, which is also subdivided into: Exus "baptized" (because they are baptized on Good Friday): these are those who are indoctrinated and who after baptism start helping their "horses5". Pagan Exus (also called Exu da Rua): they are those who do evil to people (AMARAL : 2003, p 45).

One of the central elements of Umbanda is mediunity. The medium is the intermediary between the spirit world and our reality. Therefore, it is around him that the Umbanda is organized, and it is the mediums that people seek to solve their problems. In other words, the medium is the vehicle of communication between the orixás and the faithful. In this sense, it can be said that without mediumship there is no Umbanda (Cf. SARACENI : 2003 p. 30-32).

The rituals in Umbanda, called "cute", have indispensable elements for the development of spirituality and mediumship. In the following we list some elements used in the "giras":

> **Smoking:** they discharge the vibrating field and subtract its vibrations, making it receptive to positive energies.
> **Palms:** if cadenced and rhythmic, they create a wide sound field whose sharp vibrations reach the center of the perception located in the minds of mediums.
> **Singing:**... they act on some plexuses (...) facilitating incorporation.
> **Attack and other instruments:** Sound vibrations have the power to numb the emotional, stimulate the perceptional, alter the energetic radiations and act on the vibratory pattern of the medium.
> **Dance:** Umbanda and Candomblé resort to "ritual dances" (...) the cadenced movement facilitates their involvement and their incorporation by their spiritual guide. (SARACENI: 2003, 43).

Like Candomblé, Umbanda is also worth the offerings. They are understood as a demonstration of respect and faith and ensure that the deities care for and care for the people they have offered with faith (Cf. SARACENI: 2003, p. 217).

Religions with African roots developed in Brazil for several centuries and continue to incorporate values of Brazilian culture in their manifestations of faith, because the religious formation of Afro-Brazilians is confused with the very formation of Brazilian society. They are religions used to accompany their followers to where they migrate. Therefore, Candomblé and Umbanda have a particularity of adaptation that allows these religions to be present throughout Brazil. So, do they exist in the North of Brazil, did they reach Boa Vista - Roraima?

Our attempts to answer these questions will be presented in the next chapter.

CHAPTER III

3. FIELDWORK: MAPPING OF YARDS IN GOOD VIEW.

The capital of the state of Roraima, Boa Vista, is the most populous municipality in the state, housing more than 60% of the entire population of Roraima and continues to attract, constantly, new immigrants, both from the rural area of the state and from other units of the federation, mainly northeastern, Amazonian and Para, and even from neighboring countries Venezuela and Guyana. We chose Boa Vista as a field of study because it constitutes a complex space and because it has a fascinating cultural mix, the result of an intense migratory flow.

3.1 - CHARACTERISTICS OF THE FIELD STUDIED.

The municipality of Boa Vista was the first town with an urban characteristic in the current state of Roraima that was formed still in the 19th century. From the 50's, from that century on, countless farms were established in the savannas that mark the high course of Rio Branco and, in 1858, the Government of the State of Amazonas created the Parish of Nossa Senhora do Carmo that, 32 years later, was elevated to the category of municipality, by the state decree No. 49 of July 9, 1890, signed by the governor of the State of Amazonas, Augusto Ximeno de Villeroy, with the name of Boa Vista do Rio Branco. The installation of the municipality was carried out by Captain Fábio Barreto Leite, on July 25, 1890. (FREITAS : 2001, 65 and www.boavista.rr.gov.br 05.03.07).

On September 13, 1943, by decree 5,812, the municipality (increased by some lands in the extreme south) was dismembered from the state of Amazonas and transformed into the Federal Territory of Rio Branco. Boa Vista became the territory's capital in 1944. In 1962, the Territory received the name of Federal Territory of Roraima and, finally, with the Constitution of 1988, it was elevated to the category of State. (www.boa.vista, 05.03.07).

Boa Vista is located at 2° 49' 17" north latitude and 60° 9' 50" west longitude and is at an altitude of 90 meters above sea level. It is bordered to the north by the municipalities of Normandia, Pacaraima and Amajari, to the south by the municipalities of Mucajaí and Cantá, to the east by the municipalities of Bonfim, Cantá and Normandia and to the west by the municipality of Alto Alegre (FREITAS : 2001, p 65-68).

To understand the occupation of Roraima and the formation of the city of Boa Vista we must remember that, until 1943, Roraima was part of the state of Amazonia and that, until 1977, the access to its center, Boa Vista, was only possible through the Rio Branco, navigable only for 3 to 4 months of the year. Only with the opening of the BR 174 highway and the garimpo boom in the 80's and especially in the 90's, the non-Indian population of Roraima passes the mark of 60 thousand of which, already at that time, two thirds were living in Boa Vista. According to IBGE data, in 1950, Boa Vista had 5,132 inhabitants. This number rose to 36,464 in 1970, and in 1980, the city already had 67,017, a number that jumped until 1991 to 217,583 inhabitants. In 2000 IBGE counted 200,567, a number that in 2006 grew to (estimated) 249,655[8] (FREITAS: 2001, 28 and IBGE, 2000).

In 2000, the IBGE (2000) registered 7,504 people who declared themselves black in Boa Vista, 54.6% of the total self-declared "black" in Roraima. Of this universe of people, merely 66 informed the IBGE that they were of the "Candomblé" religion and 12 presented themselves as "Umbandistas", that is: according to the data presented, in 2000, only 78 people identified themselves with religions with African matrices. This means that 1.03% of the people who declared themselves "black" declared to preserve intimate and active relations with the Afro-Brazilian religious culture in Boa Vista.

The initial objective of this research was to locate the place(s) where these 78 Afro-Brazilians practiced the religion to which they declared themselves to belong. In the 50 neighborhoods that comprise the municipality of Boa Vista (www.boavista, 05.03.07), the systematic mapping of Candomblé and Umbanda "terreiros" was done in order to make them more visible and, on the other hand, to know the persistence in the cultivation of African traditions of many Afro-Brazilians who came to Boa Vista.

3.2 - RESEARCH DEVELOPMENT.

The field research began in mid-October 2006, with some incursions into the neighborhoods of Boa Vista, in order to locate evidence that might reveal the existence of Candomblé or Umbanda terreiros, such as a white flag hoisted on bamboo in front of the house. The success of this first stage was crucial in order to establish the first contact with religious

---

[8]Cf. information from the website www.ibge.gov.br-ibege-cidades@. 01.03.07

expressions with African matrices, so that research could continue. At no point in the research was there any pretension to establish a deep coexistence with the community of terreiros, and the eventual discoveries would not serve to elaborate a research on Afro-Brazilian rituals. But the main objective of the research is to bring out an Afro-Brazilian universe that is scrambled in good society.

Thus, the first white flag hoisted on bamboo was located in the Bairro São Vicente. It was a sign that the incursions were giving their first results in locating cult grounds with African matrices. After the white flag was found, I tried to make contact with the leader of the terreiro, I looked for him in a house located next to the construction that apparently would be the Terreiro. After my presentation as a student at the Federal University of Roraima and an explanation of the purpose of my research on the mapping of the yards in the city of Boa Vista, a man who identified himself as a Bokulê father approached me and proposed to help me in my research by indicating some yards located in the Liberdade neighborhood and Tancredo Neves, inviting me to visit his yard on another occasion.

The visit to Pai Bokulê opened the doors to an unexpected universe of yards, as he informed the existence and location of several Umbanda and Candomblé yards in Boa Vista, showing that there is a network of relationships between them. Thus, after Pai Bokulê's indications, the result was a grateful enlargement of the terreiros universe. As the initial expectation was to find at most two or three, maybe even half a dozen terreiros, it was exceeded with each information obtained in the terreiros located and visited. It was then necessary to organize the visits by neighborhood, starting with those that were close to São Vicente Neighborhood and extending to the peripheral neighborhoods.

The purpose of the visitation is to collect qualitative information through informal conversations, with pre-established questions about the time of activity on site, time of initiation, number of participating members and festivities that are held in the yards. All this information has been recorded in my field notebook. An important aspect noticed during the visit process was the willingness of the fathers and mothers of the saint to answer the questions and, after the conversation, I usually received the invitation to return and participate in the terreiro festivities, especially the feast of Saint Sebastian which is celebrated on January 20th.

During the visits it was observed that the terreiros have the habit of visiting each other during the parties dedicated to the orixá that is the guide of the terreiro. This apparently facilitated the discovery of new terreiros, because with each conversation with a mother or father of a saint one obtained a list of terreiros that were part of their relationship network that could be visited later. But, on the other hand, some of the information was inaccurate, only indicating the Neighborhood and the proximity of the location of the yard, indicating the name of the mother or father, which made it difficult to locate the yard. One of the best sources of information, which was presented during the fieldwork, was the Terreiro de Santa Bárbara, which considerably expanded the addresses of the terreiro to be visited.

The target to be reached with the visits are the mothers and fathers of saints, because the dynamics of the terreiro pulsates around the religious leadership exercised by them. The importance of the father and mother of saints consists in their being the repositories and transmitters of the knowledge about the religious practices of the African matrix cults. According to the father Totó, of Terreiro Santa Bárbara, it is not the person who chooses to become the father and mother of a saint, but it is the orixás who make this choice through illness, unhappiness in love, or other form of persuasion. Therefore, each father and mother of a saint only follows the will of the orixá and fulfills his obligations as a caretaker of the orixás.

So that the investigation would not become a mere collection of data and would become a participating investigative process, I attended some festivities of some terreiros: São Sebastião party in the terreiro of Maria de Oxossi; Sábado de Aleluia in Terreiro Santa Bárbara and Ogum de Ronda. Another technique used to obtain information about the characteristics of the terreiros was photography. The photos were made in sony digital camera with a resolution of 3 Megapixels. In this way, all the yards have a photographic record[9] that reveals some external aspects, such as facades, and internal aspects, such as the settlement of orixás and private altars of each yard.

The challenge of this investigation was to get rid of any prejudice, because much is unknown about African religious practices and many myths are built about yards, dispatches and the fathers and mothers of saints. Another barrier to be overcome in the location of the terreiros was the fact that a large number of terreiros have no visible external indication and therefore go unnoticed by most people who travel the streets of the neighborhoods. In addition, the Terreiros are located on the same grounds as the homes of the fathers of santo or mothers of santo. This aspect required that many neighborhoods be traveled street by street during the mapping period, which began in the second half of October 2006 and was completed in the second half of March 2007.

3.3 - THE AFRICAN MATRIX TERREIROS IN GOOD VIEW.

---

[9] During the research, some terreiros did not allow the use of the camera, so there is not 100% of the universe registered in photos. The photos are in my private archive and part in appendix A.

As we walk through the neighborhoods of Boa Vista, we observe that there is an Afro-Brazilian universe that can go unnoticed by the less attentive gaze or those who insist on denying that the African cultural presence is part of the city's daily life. But the white flags[10] hoisted on bamboo indicate that in several places people gather to worship the orixás in Candomblé and Umbanda terreiros. However, not all of the terreiros have the white flag hoisted, only the terreiros that have the settlement of the orixás. With this, it is common to see the flags on the terreiros that have long since settled there. We can also see below the white flag a green, yellow, red or other colored flag hoisted on a smaller bamboo that indicates that in this terreiro there is also a cult to the caboclos, that is, it is a caboclo candomblé, fruit of an approach of the Candomblé with the Umbanda.

Terreiros do not always have an identification with the name visible on the facade. But another fundamental characteristic is used to identify the terreiro, the existence of a lot of vegetation and trees, in the patio of the houses, can be used as criteria to find a terreiro in Boa Vista. For example, at the entrance of the father Bokulê's yard there are two coconut trees, brought from Bahia. According to Pai Bokulê, this plant is originally from Africa and its seedlings were brought in slave ships, as they are sacred leaves from Xangô[11]. The plants are part of the terreiros because they are very important for the African religiosity, because the leaves release axé essential for life and harmony in the universe.

The terreiros are usually built in masonry, but some with less resources are built in wood. Here it is worth remembering that there is a differentiation between Candomblé and Umbanda terreiros. In the courtyard of the Candomblé terreiro there are the settlements of the orixás, the house of the Ancestrais, the house of Exu and the gira, there is a room dedicated to the initiated that cannot be visited by people who have not been initiated. The drums and atabaque have a specific place and the public is around the space of the gira which is delimited by a small wall. Where the terreiro is located there is a special room for the caboclo Candomblé, where people are served and the patio of the terreiro is large so that it can accommodate people who visit the Terreiro on the occasion of parties. In Umbanda there are no orixá settlements, because in Umbanda there is no sacrifice of animals, indispensable for the settlement of the orixás. But in the four corners of the terreiro there is the altar of the caboclos, the old black, the orixás and the central altar. There is also a special room so that people can consult with the

---

[10] The White Flag is the identification of the orixá of the time, see photo in appendix A Terreiro Oxossi p 52 and photo white flag p 67.
[11] Cf. Father Bokulê field notebook 04.01.07.

father or mother of a saint. Another specificity of Umbanda is the cruise, dedicated to "souls", a cross located at the main entrance of the terreiro that does not exist in the Candomblé terreiros.

Another aspect that attracts attention inside the yards are the colored silk paper flags that serve as a forum and decoration of the space. The colors of the flags symbolize the orixás, because each orixá is identified by its color. For example: Oxalá-white, Iansã-yellow, Oxossi-verde, Iemanjá-blue, Ogum-blue.[12] The flags are removed during Lent, when there are no activities in the yards, and new ones are placed on the occasion of the resumption of the festivities on the Saturday of Alleluia. Some terreiros have paintings of the orixás inside, these paintings were observed especially in Terreiro Ogum de Ronda[13], Templo de Iansã and Santa Bárbara.

In the Terreiros there is an overvaluation of the symbols, being common to notice inside them several religious icons arranged in altars, orixás settlements and colored flags that carry an incalculable range of information for the community dynamics. Therefore:

> (...) sacred symbols work to synthesize a people's *ethos-the* tone, character and quality of their lives, their style and moral and aesthetic arrangements-and their worldview-the picture they make of what things are today, their most comprehensive ideas about order. In religious belief and practice, the *ethos* of a group becomes intellectually reasonable because it demonstrates a type of life ideally suited to the current state of affairs that the world view describes, while this world view becomes emotionally convincing because it is presented as an image of a true state of affairs, especially well-ordered to accommodate such a type of life. (GEERTZ : 1989 p. 104).

In this way, Terreiros are guardians of a tradition and perpetuators of a perception of the world which, independent of territorial space, are passed down from generation to generation. For this reason there is a historical commitment of the fathers and mothers of saints to transmit and perpetuate the knowledge received from their ancestors.

The activities of the terreiros have several particularities. Some terreiros have frequent "touches", while others, only sporadically perform their festivities. Usually, there are "touches" in the yards fortnightly or once a month. Besides these "touches", there are special festivities dedicated to the orixás guides of the yard. The main festivities are: Iemanjá/Nossa Senhora on January 1st, Oxossi/São Sebastião on January 20th, Ibeji/Cosme and Damião on September 27th, Iansã/Santa Bárbara on December 4th and Santa Luzia on December 13th. Alcoholic drinks and food are part of the festivities, as they are also offered to the orixás. The festivities

---

[12] See also SARACENI, Op. Cit, p. 178.
[13] See Appendix A photo of Terreiro Ogum de Ronda p 51 and photo of Terreiro Templo de Iansã p 66.

are opportunities for people to visit the terreiros, as the terreiros are open to all people in the neighborhood and friendly people. Commonly during the festivities the terreiro receives visits from Pais de Santo from other terreiros that are part of the network. The festivities usually start at 8pm and go until 2am, but they can also extend until dawn, because it depends a lot on the father and mother of the saint and the people who are attending the festival. The peculiarity is due to the Terreiro Centro Espírita Irmão Raimundo and Terreiro Tenda São Pedro/ Xangô which, differently, perform their activities during the morning.

As you walk around the city and get in touch with the Terreiros you realize that an important aspect for their community dynamics are the parties. According to Amaral (2000), the purpose of the festivities is to affirm or deny social values and it is a partnership between humans, the Orixás and other deities. Therefore, the festivals in Terreiros consolidate the relations, reaffirm the associations and express world views. The parties are ways of showing what the group is and thinks. Therefore, the parties in the terreiros function as a device of visibility, because the touch of the drum and the movement around the terreiros show to the society that there is a group that expresses its culture. It is also in the parties that the networks of relationships are reaffirmed and solidarity is exercised, because in the party there is much food, music and joy.

One of the striking features of the terreiros visited is the hospitality. The members of the yard take special care of the visitors, promptly providing a place to sit, drink and eat. They briefly present some rules such as not participating in the cuiras, as they are reserved for the initiated. Certain terreiros have stricter rules, such as not allowing visitors to wear black clothes and forcing people to go through a purification ritual before entering the terreiro.

The terreiros are concentrated in the suburbs,[14] mainly in Hélio Campos, Silvo Bothelho, Cambará, Caranã, Tancredo Neves and adjacent neighborhoods, that is, the neighborhoods that were created by the Roraima government in the 1980s. These data corroborate with information from Aimberê Freitas:

> The old Pintolândia 1,2,3 and 4 districts, located in the outskirts of Boa Vista, as the name indicates, were allotted and built by Ottomar in his first term as governor-elect, and are traditional redoubts in the city. (...) being evident in that redoubt the predominance of their uses and customs (SOUZA : 2005 p 265).

---

[14] See location of Terreiros on map in appendix C p. 70

However, it is not only in the periphery that the Candomblé and Umbanda terreiros are located, we can find some traditional terreiros in the neighborhoods near the center as in Mecejana, São Vicente and São Francisco.

During the location I could observe that the people in the neighborhood know the terreiros and have a certain relationship with them. Nevertheless, in some cases, I noticed a certain discomfort in the people when they were asked if they knew, in the vicinity, any yard. This shows that there is, to a certain extent, prejudice against Afro-Brazilian cults, because it is not said openly that one attends or knows the locals, but the reality is that they are part of the dynamic of the city. I was able to observe, in one of my visits, people looking for help in the yard. According to Pai Totó, there are few members of the terreiro, but there are many visitors who seek help in the work done there.[15]

During the period of the fieldwork I was able to locate 21 terreiros, of which the majority, 71% identify themselves as being from Umbanda and 29% recognize themselves as Candomblé. The nations that can be observed in the universe of Candomblé terreiros are: Angola, Ketu, and Nagô. However, even though it is Candomblé, there is Caboclo's Candomblé in the terreiro as a result of the approach to Umbanda.

CHART 1

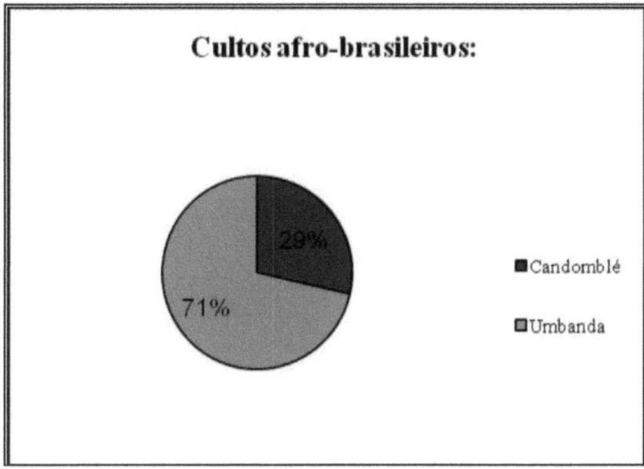

---

[15] Cf. Pai Toto, field notebook 13.01.2007.

The fathers and mothers of Santo are not from Roraima, they come from other Brazilian states, 52% have their origin in the state of Maranhão, 24% came from Amazonas and 24% come from other states of the federation. Therefore, it is evident that in the migratory process there was no loss of cultural elements, because they maintained their spiritual activity. Among the fathers and mothers of saint only the mother Silvia was "made in the saint" in Roraima, the other leaders had their initiation in Maranhão or Pará.

CHART 2

Analyzing the time that the Terreiros are in activity it can be verified that the migration of the fathers and mothers of santo suffer intervals, which can be associated with other elements that favor the migration cycles to the border regions. It was observed that 24% of the Terreiros are in activity for more than 20 years, 47% are in activity between 10 and 20 years, 19% are present in Boa Vista between 05 and 09 years and only 10% of the Terreiros mapped did not present the possibility of ascertaining the time of their activity in the city.

CHART 3

Another reality observed in the wanderings of the Terreiros is that some mothers and fathers of saints are illiterate or have low schooling, which can represent a barrier for the organization in associations and formalize actions that give visibility to their religiosity, their social importance and their cultural expression. This becomes evident when we see that only in the last two years Afro-Brazilian Cult Associations have emerged in Boa Vista. The first to appear was the Afro-Brazilian Association of Roraima, founded on 10.01.06, having as president "Mãe Sílvia" of Terreiro   Ylê Axé Oba Agodô, and the second is the Umbandist Spiritist Association and the Afro-Brazilian Cults of the State of Roraima Santa Bárbara,founded on 23.12.2006, having as president the "Pai Totó" of Terreiro Santa Bárbara. While the research was being carried out there was no news of affiliations.

Because of the low level of education of the fathers and mothers of saints and the tradition of oral transmission of knowledge in the Terreiros of cults with African matrices, Afro-Brazilian cults can fit into Geertz's classical concept of culture:

> It denotes a pattern of historically transmitted meanings embodied in symbols, a system of inherited conceptions expressed in symbolic form through which men communicate, perpetuate, and develop their knowledge and activities in relation to life. (GEERTZ : 1989p. 103)

Since one of the functions of the terreiro is to transmit its culture, it is unlikely that the number of Afro-Brazilian cult followers in Boa Vista will be only 78 as IBGE has counted. According to Silvia's mother, there are 86 supporters in her yard, so only in one yard is the IBGE number exceeded. It is evident, then, that there is a difficulty, on the part of those who attend the afros cults, to identify themselves as practitioners of Candomblé and Umbanda. This shows that the issue of discrimination and prejudice is part of our society in the social and cultural games that qualify some people as better and others as not being citizens. In the second category are Afro-Brazilian people who practice the African matrix cults. We see that people who attend the terreiros do not have the freedom to identify themselves as members of Candomblé or Umbanda.

The above issues are enough to justify the problem that Afro-Brazilian people have to become visible in Brazilian and Roraim society, and make their cultural traditions known and respected. Therefore, it is by the pattern of social behavior in Roraima that Afro-Brazilians are made invisible in the political and social sphere. However, it is evident from the mapping of 21 terreiros in Boa Vista that there is an Afro-Brazilian reality pulsating within the social hierarchy of the municipality.

Now the challenge remains to bring from marginality to the center of the anthropological debate in Roraima the issues pertinent to the black culture of Roraima, so that the negative factor that, throughout history, has become the identification of African roots for Afro-Brazilians can be deconstructed and thus broaden the debate on the social inclusion of Afro-Brazilians in the social policies of the state as the indigenous issue has been addressed today.

The discovery of 21 terreiros in Boa Vista reveals that there is a rich universe of information for anthropology to discover new paths for the construction of its "knowledge" in the extreme north of the country. For we can only understand this society if we can bring to light its own way of being, living and conceiving the world. In order to perceive the anthropological issues related to Afro-descendants we need to blur our gaze so that we can unravel the mystery of the cultural mosaic that is Roraima.

I realize that this mapping can indicate paths for the development of new research that are able to elucidate the cultural issues of Afro-Brazilians who migrated to Boa Vista and continue to build their identity. Of course, these new researches should not follow the old axiom of Western superiority, which looks down on these people from above, let alone fall into the traps of the theory of "racial democracy".

Therefore, I believe that the result of this research is a practical support for the development, in the anthropological exercise, of a study group on the issues related to Afro-descendant culture at UFRR. I remember that in Roraima we find not only Afro-Brazilians, but also Afro-descendants from countries that border the state.

CONCLUDING REMARKS

Locating and mapping the Candomblé and Umbanda terraces is based on the assumption that people from the Northeast of Brazil preserve and currently practice their religiosity. Therefore, mapping would bring out the cultural and religious manifestation of a part of the goodist population that is not easily perceived by the general society. In this way the mapping would contribute to a greater social visibility of the Terreiros and their visitors.

The municipality of Boa Vista has 50 Neighbourhoods and during the mapping period all the Neighbourhoods were visited and 21 terreiros were located in them, most of which 71% identify themselves as being from Umbanda and 29% recognise themselves as Candomblé. The Terreiros are concentrated in the peripheral neighbourhoods, formerly known as Pintolândias, which today are: Alvorada, Senator Hélio Campos, Dr. Silvio Leite and Santa Luzia. However, there are also terreiros in the more central neighborhoods such as São Vicente, São Francisco and Mecejana.

One of the oldest terreiros and that exerts a certain influence on the other terreiros located in the old Pintolândia neighborhoods is the Terreiro Santa Bárbara do Bairro Cambará. This is where the Umbandist Spiritist Association and the Afro-Brazilian Cults of the State of Roraima Santa Bárbara works. Besides the Santa Bárbara Association, there is in Roraima the Afro-Brazilian Association of Roraima, founded on January 10, 2006 that is presided by the mother Silvia do Terreiro YLÊ AXÉ OBA AGODÔ (King Xangô's Power House), located in Bairro Caranã. Some Candomblé terreiros are affiliated to associations outside Roraima, such as Terreiro Alaguinã Axé Abeocuta - Fon which is affiliated to the federation of Belém - PA.

Few terreiros had ties with associations. This is because the Associations in Boa Vista are in the process of formation and membership. There is also some resistance among the leaderships against the idea of joining, as this could mean "losing freedom", that is, autonomy. On the other hand, the emergence of two associations reveals that there is a certain dissonance between Candomblé and Umbanda. This fact could be analyzed in more depth to discover the reasons that led both groups to form an independent association.

Another factor to be taken into account for the fragile organization of the Terreiros is its recent history in Roraima, because only with the "garimpo boom" in the 1980s did the Afro-Brazilian population migrate substantially to the state. This is evident when one realizes that 67% of the Terreiros have from 05 years to 20 years of activity. This reality is determinant for the articulation of a more effective organization in the representation of the terreiros at the level of political struggles in Boa Vista.

According to the information of the 21 fathers and mothers of saints who were located in this mapping, the number of fixed members of the yards in Boa Vista would reach the number of 344 people, apart from the people who are adepts of the afros cults, but are not fixed members of the yards.

As one travels through the neighborhoods of Boa Vista, one realizes that they guard, with great propriety, the culture of the diverse populations that conform them. In each neighborhood, where a Terreiro was found and mapped, we observe the magical opening of the curtains of a rich cultural universe, which values what costs more to its inhabitants, the religiosity. Even if the comprehensive society insists on not perceiving the existence of an afro pulsar in Boa Vista, it reveals itself by the more attentive look of those who walk the streets of the city's neighborhoods.

It is true that the Terreiros visited are quite distinct from each other. There are some with unmistakable signs of identification, in general they are also the most structured. On the other hand, there are small terreiros, without identification, and with precarious infrastructure. But there is something that unites them: the network of friendship. For when there is a party in one of them, the members of the others visit it in solidarity. This causes the big terreiros and the small ones to be taken by the same glamour in the festivities of "their" respective Orixás. In this sense, all the Terreiros play the role of perpetuating a single cultural and religious tradition, strengthening the bonds between the fraction of the population of Boa Vista who practice the religions with African matrices.

The Afro-Brazilian religiosity has little notoriety or visibility in the daily life of this city, especially for those, the vast majority of the Good Visitors, who do not know how to "read" the signs with which the bearers of it communicate their presence among themselves. The terreiros themselves struggle, not so much for more "visibility", but for social recognition, as a cultural expression proper to a people that is part of the geography of the city. But in this they encounter some problems, specifically the illiteracy of the leaders, because during the visits I could observe that the majority of fathers and mothers of saints have low schooling. They were illiterate or functionally illiterate. Therefore, without formal school education it becomes difficult for the Terreiros populations to articulate and organize themselves in order to fight for their rights and to be able to articulate with the general society.

A major step in the search for greater notoriety of the Terreiros in Boa Vista was the creation of the two associations that have emerged in the last two years. With these initiatives the Terreiros will finally be able to obtain more space for their religious and cultural manifestations. A sign in this sense was the realization of the First Meeting of the Black Population of Roraima, for their participation as a specific sector in the State Conference of Food Security of Roraima. This meeting took place on March 15, 2007, in Terreiro Santa Bárbara,[16]in Bairro Cambará, with the presence of several representatives of the Terreiros de Umbanda and Candomblé existing in Boa Vista. On that occasion, two people were appointed to represent the black people of Roraima at the State Conference on Food Security (CESAN), held at Casa Paulo IV, from March 21 to 23, 2007[17], and consequently their names were approved to participate in the National Conference on Food Security, in Fortaleza-CE.

Our "mapping" of the Terreiros in Boa Vista itself played an important role in this process. Because, in some cases, the leaders and members of the contacted terreiros took advantage of this contact to make a communication link with CONSEA-RR (National Council of Food and Nutritional Security of Roraima) in the preparation of the State Meeting, and also to expand, strengthen and better articulate the communication network between them. In this way, this research contributed to the valorisation of Afro-Brazilians in Roraima. Our work of locating and mapping African matrix terreiros can shed light on a universe that the comprehensive society, particularly Roraima society, insists on not seeing, so that this academic effort has brought to light an "African" reality in the Northern region.

We are convinced that one cannot continue to claim that the Afro-Brazilian cultural tradition is only from some regions of Brazil and practically absent in others, particularly in the Amazon, despite the fact that one of the recognized centers of this tradition, the northeast of Brazil, constitutes, at the same time, the region that originates from the majority of the current inhabitants of the Amazon who have immigrated here in the last 50 years. It would be naïve to think that the northeastern migrants had left their religious traditions on the edge of the road that historically resisted the Atlantic and the sufferings of slavery. The cultural identity of the fathers and mothers of Santo, trained in religious practices in Maranhão, resisted the long journey to Roraima, as most of them before arriving in the state passed through that of Pará and did not leave their practices aside until today.

The discovery of 21 Terreiros in Boa Vista was more than a pleasant surprise. Besides exceeding our initial expectations, the research allowed us to dive deep into the Afro world, which was covered by the dark waters of prejudice and discrimination from a society that still systematically denies the value of Afro-Brazilian culture. With each visit to the Terreiros de

---

[16] See Appendix D p 71.
[17] See Appendix D p 72.

Candomblé and Umbanda, a black Boa Vista was unveiled, rocked by the drums and atabaques and taken over by the transcendental force of axé that accompanies the Afro people in their history.

In this sense, to look at the Terreiros is to ascertain a history of resistance and struggle, a culture rooted in the spirit of people who do not dissociate themselves from the past or from their religion, which, by the way, is born of the need to give answers to the events lived by people who have the dignity of life threatened by human and spiritual forces. Therefore, the dynamics of the Terreiros is complex and each response found will only have meaning in its moment. This must be the driving force for new research related to Afro-Brazilian culture in the North.

BIBLIOGRAPHY

ANDREWS, George Reid. **Blacks and whites in São Paulo (1888-1988).** São Paulo: EDUSC, 1998.

AMARAL, Rita de Cássi. City in Festa: the povo-de-santo (and other people) celebrate in São Paulo. In: MAGNANI, Jose Guilherme C. & TORRES, Lílian de Lucca (eds.). **The metropolis:** texts of Urban Anthropology. São Paulo : Fapesp, p 255-318, 2000.

AMARAL, Adilson Rogério do. **Pai João Spiritist Tent accounts of his history and the ritualistic, mystical and syncretic functioning.** São Paulo: Compacta, 2003.

BARBARA, Rosa Maria Susanna. **Music therapy in candomblé.** Available at: http://www.ffch.usp.br/sociologia/posgraduacao/jornadas/papers/. Accessed on June 30, 2005.

BASTIDE, Roger. Brazil land of contrasts. 10th ed. in: **Brazil body and soul collection.** Vol. II. São Paulo: Rio de Janeiro: DIFEL, 1980.

BERKENBROCK, Volney J. **The experience of the orixás:** a study of the religious experience of candomblé. Petrópolis: Voices, 1997.

CARVALHO, José Jorge de. The Afro-Brazilian sacred arts and the preservation of nature. **Anthropology Series,** Brasilia, n. 381, p. 2-19.

DAVIS, Darien J. **Afro-Brazilians today.** São Paulo: Black Seal, 2000.

FERNADES, Florestan. **Meaning of black protest.** São Paulo: Ed. Cortez, 1989.

FREITAS, Aimberê. **Geography and History of Roraima.** Boa Vista, 2001.

FUNES, Euripedes. Personal notes of the Lecture held at the UFRR Auditorium. December 11, 2006.

GEERTZ, Clifford. **The interpretation of cultures.** Rio de Janeiro: LTC, 1989.

HASENBARG. Carlos A. **Discrimination and Race Inequalities in Brazil.** In: Sociology Series Vol. 10. Rio de Janeiro: Edições Graal, 1979.

IBGE. Demographic census, resident population by color or race. Available at: http://www.sidra.ibge.gov.br >. Accessed in: August. 2006.

IBGE. Population of Boa Vista. Available at: www.ibge.gov.br-ibege-cidades@. Accessed on March 1st, 2007.

MAE/USP. Africa: material culture, philosophy and religion. In: **Africa:** Culture and Society. Thematic Guide for teachers. São Paulo.

RIBEIRO, Darcy. **The Brazilian people:** the formation and the meaning of Brazil. 2nd ed. São Paulo: Companhia a das Letras, 1995.

ISAIA, Arthur Caesar. Macumba in white. **Our History**, São Paulo, n. 36, p. 28-32, October 2006.

LIGIÉRO, José Luiz. **Initiation to candomblé.** 8th ed. Rio de Janeiro: Record and New Era, 2004.

LOPES, Nei. **Bantos, Maltese and black identity.** Janeir River: University Forensics, 1988.

RODRIGUES, Nina. **The Africans in Brazil. 7th** ed. Brasília: UNB Publishing House, 1988.

SANGIRARDI Jr., **God of Africa and Brazil**: Candomblé and Umbanda. Rio de Janeiro: Civilização Brasileira, 1988.

SANTILLI, Paulo. **Pemongon Pata:** Macuxi territory, conflict routes. São Paulo: UNESP Publishing House, 2001.

SARACENI, Rubens. **Doctrine and theology of a sacred umbanda**: the religion of the mysteries a hymn of love for life. São Paulo: Madras, 2003.

SILVA, Vagner Gonçalves da. The sacred corners: candomblé and the religious use of the city. In : MAGNANI, Jose Guilherme C. & TORRES, Lílian de Lucca (eds.). **The metropolis:** texts of Urban Anthropology. São Paulo: Fapesp, p 88-123, 2000.

SOUZA, Carla Monteiro de. Roriama and the Immigrations. **Texts & Debates,** Boa Vista, n. 9, p.257-271, aug. /dec. 2005.

PRANDI, Reginaldo. **The orixás and nature.** Available at: www.okitalande.com.br.orixas_natureza.htm. Accessed on: June 30, 2005.

http://www.axeoya.com.br/orixas.htm. Accessed July 1, 2005.

http://www.edeus.org/port/candomblebr.htl. Accessed July 30, 2005.

http://www.paisilvio.hpg.ig.com.br/ervasoxum.html. Accessed July 30, 2005.

http://www.thecauldronbrasil.com.br/article/view/138/1/5. Accessed June 30, 2005.

www.boavista.rr.gov.br. Accessed on March 5, 2007.

APPENDIX A

TERREIRO ÁBASSA D'ANGOLA TATA BOKULÊ

Source: Günter B. Padilha 04.01.2007
View from the entrance of Terreiro Ábassa D'angola Tata Bokulê

Source: Günter B. Padilha 04.01.2007
Orixá Settlement

Terreiro ÁBASSA D'ANGOLA TATA BOKULÊ (House of the black force of the son and father of the hunter), of the Angola Nation - Candomblé. It is located at Sorocaima Street, corner with Uraricuera n° 216, in Bairro São Vicente and has as Pai-de-santo Bokulê, native of Manaus - AM. The two trees in front are acocô, brought from Bahia. According to Pai Bokulê this plant is originally from Africa and its seedlings were brought in slave ships, because they are sacred leaves from Xangô.

TERREIRO OGUM DE RONDA

Source Günter B. Padilha 10.03.2007

Entrance of the Ogum de Ronda yard with settlement of the Orixá do tempo

Source Günter B. Padilha 10.03.2007

Altar and paintings of orixás inside the Terreiro

Terreiro Ogum de Ronda- Umbanda is located at Rua: N 13 Q 232, 1939 - Senador Hélio Campos, has 13 years of activities and his main parties are: January 20: Oxossi/ São Sebastião, June 24: Xangô, August 15: Janaina, October 28: Zé Pelinta and December 8: Ogum. The terreiro has 10 fixed members and receives an average of 60 visitors and is open to the public on Saturdays from 19:00 - 02:00. The Mother of the Saint is Mrs. Antonia Maria da Conceição "Goiabana - Adigina".

OXOSSI LANDFORM

Source Günter B. Padilha 20.01.. 2007
Oxossi Terreiro entrance, settlement of the Orixá do Tempo with fruit.

Source Günter B. Padilha 20.01.2007
Inside the Terreiro with leaves scattered on the floor

Terreiro Oxossi- Umbanda is located in: Rua Agnelo Bittencourt, 1212 - São Francisco, is 30 years in activities and its main sane parties: January 01: Iemanjá, January 20: Oxossi, April 23 São Jorge, May 13: Preto Velho, June 23: São João and September 27: Cosme e Damião.

Terreiro has 10 fixed members and receives an average of 50 visitors when it is open to the public on Saturdays from 8:00 pm to 24:00 pm. The leadership of Terreiro is exercised by Mãe-de-Santo Maria José de Oliveira - "Maria do Oxossi", born in Fortaleza - CE and started in Porto Velho - RO at 43 years old. The Terreiro is identified by Flags in the color of the orixás, in the entrance there are bushes and flowers, the interior is ample where the dances in circle are carried out, where the orixás are manifested, there is a space dedicated to the drums that is on the right side of the central altar, on the right side of the entrance door is the altar dedicated to Preto Velho and on the left side is the altar dedicated to the caboclos. The terreiro is not affiliated to any Afro-Brazilian cult association.

ANCIENT MESSENGERS OF PEACE

Source Günter B. Padilha 20.01.2007

Altar of the Cute Dove in the Yard Messengers of Peace

The Terreiro Mensageiros da Paz- Umbanda, is located at Rua: Agnelo Bittencourt, 1354 - Bairro São Francisco, is 15 years in activity under the leadership of Mãe-de-Santo Iromar Anselmo de Queiroz, natural of Itaurama-MG. The attendance to the public happens every Monday and Thursday from 20:00 to 24:00. Currently Terreiro has 30 fixed members and receives the visit of approximately 80 people. Its main parties are: January 1st: Iemanjá, January 20th: Oxossi, April 23rd: Ogum/ Pomba Gira, May 13th: Preto Velho, August 19th: Pomba Gira Cigana and September 27th: Cosme e Damião.

According to Mother Iromar the main characteristics of her yard are: "Umbanda of the Kardecista line, does not play the drums inside the yard, only in some parties the drum is played in the yard. Every Monday and Thursday the terreiro has pass works, counseling, bath preparations and unloading".

The yard has no visible identification and is small, located in the back of Dona Iromar's house. From the entrance door of the one to locate the central altar, to your left and there is a small room for Exu's "dispatches" works. On the right side of the door there is a red velvet chair where the Dove Gira incorporates and advises people. At parties it is used for alcoholic drinks (beer). The first location of the terreiro was near the Folha de Boa Vista Newspaper, on Rua Antônio Augusto Martins. The terreiro is not affiliated to any Afro-Brazilian cult association. When there is a party it is common for the Terreiro to receive visits from Pai de Santos and members of other terreiros in the city.

NAGÔ MINE BARBARIAN HOLY TENT

Source Günter B. Padilha 20.01.2007

Altar of Iemanjá in Seara Tenda Santa Bárbara Mina

Seara Tenda Santa Bárbara Mina Nagô- Umbanda, located at Av. São José, 602 - Alvorada, has been in activity for 06 years, its main parties are: 01 January: Iemanjá, 20 January: Oxossi/ São Sebastião, 04 October: São Francisco, 27 September: Cosme e Damião and 13 December: Santa Luzia. The attendance to its 08 fixed members and the 20 visitors takes place every fortnight on Saturdays from 20:00 to 24:00. The leadership of the terreiro is in charge of Mãe-de-santo: Maria de Jesus Silva - "Maria de Jesus", born in Esperantinópolis - MA, was initiated 30 years ago, in Brejo de Areia - MA.

Second Mother Mary of Jesus: her yard is called "seara" because it has no drum. That is why the cute ones are animated by the clapping of the hands of the participants. The works of the yard are of prayers, baths, bottles and counseling. The cute ones happen every fortnight. Mary of Jesus is also a midwife, as she says: "I have the gift to trim the children". Before Roraima came, she had a yard in the city of Itaituba - PA. The yard is of a singular simplicity, built in wood, located in the back of the house. Walking along the avenues you do not notice the existence of the yard, because there is no identification. In the backyard there are hoses and some bushes. The interior of the yard is similar to the other yards, with space for dancing and altars. The terreiro is in the process of joining the recently formed Associação Culto Afro-brasileiro Santa Bárbara. Dona Maria de Jesus is Ritual Supervisor of the Association.

HOLY BARBARA

Source Günter B. Padilha 10.03.2007
Façade of Terreiro Santa Barbara

Source Günter B. Padilha 27.01.2007
Cute in Terreiro Santa Barbara

Terreiro Santa Barbara - Umbanda is located at Rua: Armando Nogueira,2997 - Cambará, has 21 years of activity. Its main parties are: January 1st: Iemanjá, January 20th: Oxossi/ São Sebastião, October 4th: São Francisco, September 27th: Cosme e Damião, December 13th: Santa Luzia. The Terreiro is open to the public on the third Saturday of the month from 8pm to 2pm. The Terreiro has 10 fixed members and receives around 60 visitors. The leader of the Terreiro is Pai Totó- Antônio Vitorino da Conceição from Caxias - MA, initiated by Zé Bruna Nazaré, and president of the Associação Culto Afro-Brasileiro Santa Bárbara, of which the Terreiro is the headquarters. The Terreiro has a large room for the gira showing that it is well frequented, has altars in the four corners, like the other terreiros visited, and a special place for women to change clothes.

TERREIRO SÃO JORGE (OGUM)

Source Günter B. Padilha 20.01.2007
Façade of Terreiro São Jorge (Ogum)

Source Günter B. Padilha 20.01.2007
Altar of Terreiro São Jorge (Ogum)

The Terreiro São Jorge (Ogum) - Umbanda is located at Rua: Antônio Batista Miranda , 912 - Equatorial, but it cannot be observed by those who pass by the street, as it is located at the back of the residence of the Mother of Saint "Fátima São Jorge" - Maria de Fátima Pereira Aragão. The terreiro has existed for 11 years and has as main parties: January 20: Oxossi/ São Sebastião, September 27: Cosme and Damião, December 13: Santa Luzia. Its activities take place once a month, but without a fixed date from 7pm to 2am. The terreiro has 12 fixed members and receives the visit of approximately 40 people for the activities. Mother Fatima is a native of Teresina - PI, was started 45 years ago in the city of Itaituba- PA by Maria de Jesus Silva.

TERREIRO SANTA BARBARA (Pintolândia neighborhood)

Source Günter B. Padilha 13.01.2007
Façade of Terreiro Santa Barbara

Source Günter B. Padilha 13.01.2007
Altar of Preto-Velho in Terreiro Santa Barbara

Terreiro Santa Bárbara- Umbanda is located in freight to the health post of Praça Germano in Pitolândia, at Rua N-8 casa 736. It has 10 years of activities and its main parties are: January 20: Oxossi/ São Sebastião, August 30: São Raimundo, September 27: Cosme e Damião, October 4: São Francisco and December 4: Santa Bárbara. Its activities are from 8:00 pm - 24:00 pm where 09 fixed members and numerous visitors participate. The leader of Terreiro is Mother "Maria das Graças" - Maria das Graças Santos Reis, born in Bacabal - Ma. The Terreiro is in the process of joining the Association. The interior of the terreiro is illustrated with Amazonian images.

TERREIRO YLE AXÉ YA PAMILADE - KETU- CANDOMBLÉ NATION

Source Günter B. Padilha 15.01.2007
View from Terreiro Yle Axé Ya Pamilade Street - Ketu- Nation

Terreiro Yle Axé Ya Pamilade is located at Rua: Guilherme Brito, 342 - Liberdade. Its main parties are: January 1st: Iemanjá, January 20th: Oxossi/ São Sebastião, October 4th: São Francisco, September 27th: Cosme e Damião, December 13th: Santa Luzia, opening hours are from 9:00pm -01:00am. With the number of 25 fixed members it still receives approximately 70 per party. The leader of Terreiro is "Pai Mario", born in Manaus - AM. The Terreiro is identified by a sign that announces the services of the terreiro and by a white flag. At the entrance there are many bushes and trees. The gira hall is large and has several orixás paintings and several Orixás settlements are located.

THE TERREIRO TENT SÃO PEDRO/ XANGÔ

Source Günter B. Padilha 15.01.2007
"The Cruise" and the Mother of Saint "Maria Maranhense"

Source Günter B. Padilha 15.01.2007
Altar of the Orixá of the children in the Terreiro Tenda São Pedro

The Terreiro Tenda São Pedro/ Xangô- Umbanda is located at Rua : Pedro Vasconcelos, 523 - Liberdade, has 27 years of activities and its main parties are: June 29 São Pedro,

September 27: Cosme e Damião, December 4: Santa Bárbara. His activities take place every Saturday from 08:00 -10:00, the only terreiro that makes his parties during the day. It has 09 fixed members and receives the visit of 20 people who are led by Maria Filomena Texeira - "Maria Maranhense", born in Santa Inês - MA and has 50 years of initiation. The Terreiro has already suffered three fires and was rebuilt to continue Maria Maranhense's obligations. He is not associated to an afro cult association.

TERREIRO ALAGUINÃ AXÉ ABEOCUTA

Source Günter B. Padilha 18.01.2007

Façade of the Terreiro Alaguinã Axé Abeocuta - Fon

The Terreiro Alaguinã Axé Abeocuta - Fon- Candomblé is located at Rua: Ivone Pinheiro, 1445 - Tancredo Neves I. With 17 years of activities I have the custom of celebrating the following parties: January 1st: Iemanjá, Oxossi/ São Sebastião, January 21st: caboclo Ita-Bandeira, Saturday of Aleluia, June 13th: Caboclo Simamba, August 31st: Exú, December 13th: Santa Luzia/ cabocla Mariana. The activities in Terreiro are from 17:00 - 22:00 for consultations and development activities of Santo and 19:00 - 04:00 for the accomplishment of the parties. There are 20 children of Santo (fixed members) and 50 visitors that participate in the dynamics of the Terreiro that is under the leadership of YATILYSA LEFAN - "Mãe zeladora de Santo", born in Manaus - AM and started (the making of Santo) in Belém - PA.

The terreiro is identified with its name on the façade, visible from the street and by the white flag, orixá of the time. There is a high punch that prevents seeing from the street the space dedicated to consultations and "cute". The terreiro is built in masonry and has a large space for performing the rituals. The house of the Mother of Saint is in the back of the yard. The terreiro also has the cult of caboclos, the cult linked to Umbanda, but with some differences of the identities they incorporate, in the candomblé are the Turks and bandeirantes and in Umbanda are the boiadeiros. The terreiro is affiliated to the federation of Belém - PA.

TERRIFIC SPIRITIST CENTER BROTHER RAIMUNDO

Source Günter B. Padilha 30.01.2007
Façade of the Terreiro Centro Espírita Brother Raimundo

Source Günter B. Padilha 30.01.2007
Father Raimundo before the Altar

The Terreiro: Centro Espírita Irmão Raimundo,- Umbanda, is located at Rua: Luiz Laranjeira, 87 corner with Rua: Quintino Level Lima- Mecejana. The Terreiro is in operation for 23 years and its main parties are: January 20: Oxossi/ São Sebastião, May 31: São

Raimundo, December 4: Santa Bárbara, December 8: Nossa Senhora da Conceição. The activities take place every fortnight from 7:30 -11:30 with 20 fixed members and 30 visitors. The leadership of Terreiro is exercised by "Pai Raimundo" - Raimundo Policarpo de Souza, born in Bacabal - MA, started 34 years ago.

TERREIRO SÃO FRANCISCO

Source Günter B. Padilha 03.03.2007

Façade of Terreiro São Francisco with the "cruise" dedicated to souls

Source Günter B. Padilha 03.03.2007

Settlement of Orixás Terreiro São Francisco

The Terreiro São Francisco - Umbanda, is located at S14 - Av. Monteiro Reias, 491 - Senador Hélio Campos, has 09 activities and have as main parties: January 20: Oxossi / São Sebastião, September 27: Cosme and Damião, their activities (drumming Tambor) take place every 20 days from 19:00 - 02:00. Currently it has 10 fixed members and approximately 15 visitors per activity. The leadership is exercised by "Mãe Francisca" - Francisca Borges da Silva "Francisca", born in Santa Luzia - MA, she was initiated 10 years ago.

Black clothing is not allowed in the yard and can only be accessed after bathing and smoking purification. The initiation of Francisca was due to illness. The São Sebastião party is held in the woods and not in the Terreiro, when the time comes for the party the whole terreiro is transplanted to the woods for the celebration. "Mother Francisca informs that the colorful flags in the Terreiro represent the orixás. This information was collected on 03/03/07.

TERREIRO OGUM ROMPE MATO

Source: Günter B. Padilha 03.03.2007
View of Exú's house

The Terreiro Ogum Rompe Mato - Umbanda and Candomblé, is located at Rua: Capitão Francisco Ferreira, 259 - Mecejana, has 28 years of activities and holds the following parties: January 27: Ogum, May 8: Preto Velho, November 25: Dona Cigana and November 29: Dona Mariana. The schedule of its activities goes from 8:00 pm to 24:00 pm. Currently there are 08 fixed members in Terreiro and approximately 15 people visit it during the parties. The leader of Terreiro is "Pai Saadi de Iemanjá", a native of Rio de Janeiro - RJ and has been in the business for 58 years.

The Terreiro is located in the back of the residence, built of masonry. There is no external identification of Terreiro. The yard belongs to Lucrecia who's sick. But it's commanded by Saadi of Iemanjá of the Fon Nation. That's why Terreiro has activities linked to Umbanda and Candomblé. On March 3, 2007, when I went to visit Terreiro Saadi of Iemanjá he was not there. The information presented here was provided by Pergigã.

TERREIRO SÃO FRANCISCO

Source Günter B. Padilha 03.03.2007
Façade of Terreiro São Francisco

The Terreiro São Francisco - Umbanda, is located for 20 years at Rua: Puraque n° 1873 - Santa Tereza II. The main festivities are: October 4th: St. Francis and Saturday of Alleluia. The "batuques" are held every fortnight with 04 fixed members and 30 visitors. The "Mãe Conceição", born in Pedreira-MA, has 40 years of initiation.

The construction of masonry, painted white and with a visible cruise through some bushes, reveals the existence of the Terreiro. However, there is no identification of the Terreiro that is next to the residence of "Mãe Conceição".

"Mother Conceição" was feeling uncomfortable with my presence and therefore did not allow the entrance to the yard, only an external photo of the yard.

TERREIRO YLÊ AXÉ OBA AGODÔ

Source Günter B. Padilha 04.03.2007
Façade of Terreiro YLÊ AXÉ OBA AGODÔ

Source Günter B. Padilha 04.03.2007
Settlement of Exú in Terreiro YLÊ AXÉ OBA AGODÔ

The Terreiro YLÊ AXÉ OBA AGODÔ (King Xangô's Powerhouse)- Candomblé - Nação Ketu, is located at Rua: Soldado Gudivaldo, 102 - Caranã and has 12 years of activities. The main parties held in the terreiro are: February 10: Maria Padilha (Gira dove), April 20: José Raimundo (Boiadeiro), June 23: Xangô - (São João Batista),July 14: Júlio Galego (sailor),October 11: Ciganas. Activities start at 8:00pm and end at 24:00pm. The Terreiro has 88 fixed members and 100 people visit him on the occasion of the festivities. The leadership is exercised by "Mãe Sílvia" - Severiano Miranda de Oliveira Silva, born in Óbidos - PA and has 38 years of initiation.

There's no I.D. that makes it possible to locate the Terrero from the street. But people in the neighborhood know Terreiro and give the information to get to him. Mother Silvia" was made in the saint in Roraima, where she has lived since she was two years old. In previous years she had terreiro in the city of São Luís do Anauá - RR and in Parintins -AM. Currently he is the President of the Afro-Brazilian Association of Roraima, founded on January 10, 2006.

YANSAN TEMPLE

Source: Günter B. Padilha 10.03.2007
Façade of the Terreiro Temple of Iansã

Source: Günter B. Padilha 10.03.2007
Drums in the Iansã Temple Yard

The Terreiro Templo de Iansã - Umbanda, is located at Rua: N 15 com S 17- Hélio Campos for 07 years and has these parties: 01 de Janeiro: Iemanjá, 20 de janeiro: Oxossi/ São Sebastião, 29 de junho: São Pedro, 03 de dezembro: Iansã. His activities start at 5pm and finish at 7am. The fixed members are a total of 14 and the visitors are approximately 70 people. The leader of Terreiro is "Mãe Quina Bomborosi" - Francisca Silva de Sousa, born in Venturino Filho - MA and 43 years ago she was initiated in the saint. A white flag hoisted in bamboo and a sign on the facade of the terreiro facilitates its location.

White Flag

Source: Günter B. Padilha 03.03.2007
White Flag "Orixá do Tempo"

The white flag located at Rua: Estrela Dalva - Raiar do Sol indicates that an Afro-Brazilian Terreiro de culto works here. However, it was not possible to make contact with the leaders of this place. According to information from "Mãe Ossilene" (02.14.07), this is a Candomblé Terreiro and is being led by "Mãe Maria Helena" who lives in Manaus-AM.

APPENDIX B

NO PHOTO INFORMATION

The Terreiro Oxossi- Umbanda, is located at Rua Carmelo, 93 - Sílvio Botelho, has 09 years of activities and its main parties are: January 20th: Oxossi, February   6th: Cabocla Brava, February 28th: Cabocla Tereza Légua, March 27th: Caboclo Sibamba, September 27th: Cosme e Damião, November 18th: Caboclo Ubirajara, December 8th: Cabocla Mariana. The activity in Terreiro takes place every Saturday from 8:30 pm - 24:00 pm with 25 members in attendance and approximately 50 guests. The leadership in Terreiro is of "Mae Osilene" - Osilene Garcia Márquez, born in Borba - AM, was initiated 27 years ago.

The small wooden yard, painted green, is in front of the house of the mother of the saint, at the end of Carmelo Street. There is little space to make the turns, so they are held in the courtyard of the Terreiro. In the middle of Terreiro there are all the altars that exist in other terreiros. There are not many plants around Terreiro. According to Osilene, the Terreiro worked for eight years at the beginning of Carmelo Street and was bigger than the current one. Information collected on 14.02.07.

Seara de Oxalá- Umbanda, is located at Rua Dona Cota Vieira n° 1239- Caimbé, has 10 years of activities and the attendance to the public is from Monday to Friday from 08:00 - 12:00 and from 13:00-18:00. At Seara there are no parties, only letter readings and healing rituals. Seara is led by "Mãe Zilmar" - Zilmar Pereira Borges, born in Santa Inês -MA and started 21 years ago.

At Seara there are no fixed members, only visitors who seek the works of clairvoyance and healing. It is located in the back of Zilmar's residence, it consists of a small unpainted wooden room with some ferns hanging from the outside wall, some chickens running loose in the yard. Inside there is an altar and several images of saints. There is no indication that can identify Seara to the people who pass by the street, but the people in the neighborhood know where Ms. Zilmar attends. Ms. Zilmar informed that her Seara, previously, was located near the Buriti fair. Before coming to Roraima, Ms. Zilmar worked in the city of Itaituba in Pará.

Another important detail reported by Ms. Zilmar is that during Lent she makes chains of prayers every Friday, so on this occasion it is not opportune to visit her.

Tereiro São Jorge - Umbanda/Quimbanda, is located at Rua: Zuldimar Saraiva de Pinho, 636- 18 com a V - Jardim Caranã, approximately 12 years old. Its main parties are: January 1st:

Iemanjá, January 20th: Oxossi/ São Sebastião, May 8th: Preto Velho, September 27th: Cosme e Damião, September 23rd: Nego Gerson, October 27th: Chica baiana. The fixed members of Terreiro are 32 and a further 100 people dress him regularly at the time of his activities from 8:00 pm to 1:30 am. The leadership of Terreiro is in charge of "Mãe Conceição Loura", born in Bacabal - MA and 45 years old.

Dona Conceição did not allow the yard to be seen, much less allowed it to be photographed. It remains a mystery, a curiosity to see what this yard looks like. The information was collected on 04.03.07

APPENDIX C

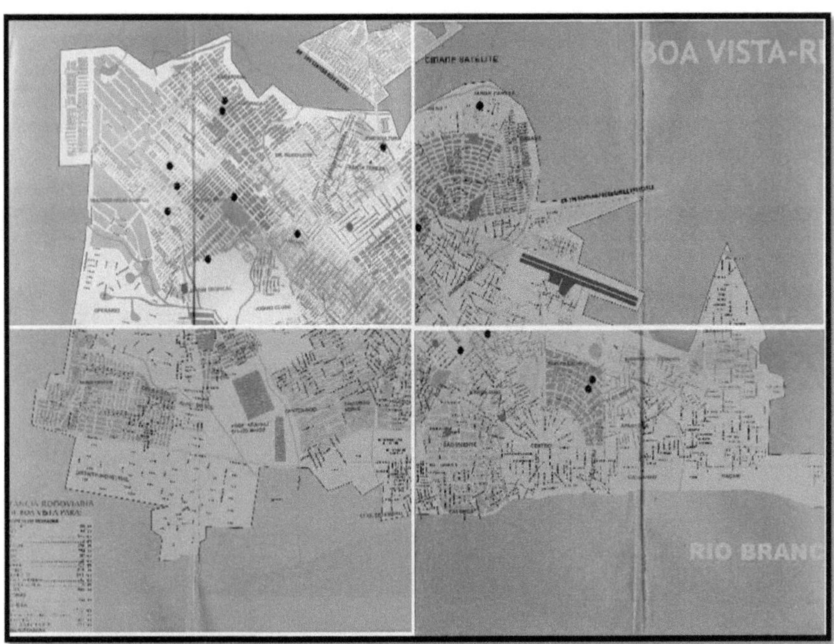

Map of the City of Boa Vista with the location of the Umbanda and Candomblé yards

APPENDIX D

I MEETING OF THE BLACK POPULATION OF RORRAIMA

Source: Günter B. Padilha 15.03.2007

Group discussion on the importance of Terreiros in food security.

Source: Günter Bayerl Padilha, 15.03.2007

Daughters of Saint

STATE FOOD SECURITY CONFERENCE - GOOD VIEW -RR

Source: Günter B. Padilha 21.03.2007
Opening Act of the Conference at the Palace of Culture

Source: Günter Bayerl Padilha. 22.03.2007
Lecture : "The Black Question in Roraima", given by the Social Sciences academic of the UFRR of Neygila Santos, during the Conference at Casa Paulo VI.

Printed by Books on Demand GmbH, Norderstedt / Germany